Setting for the South Street Theatre production of "Cahoots." Set design by Scott Bradley.

CAHOOTS

A Comedy in Two Acts

BY RICK JOHNSTON

★

DRAMATISTS
PLAY SERVICE
INC.

CAHOOTS
Copyright © 1990, Rick Johnston

All Rights Reserved

CAUTION: Professionals and amateurs are hereby warned that performance of CAHOOTS is subject to a royalty. It is fully protected under the copyright laws of the United States of America, and of all countries covered by the International Copyright Union (including the Dominion of Canada and the rest of the British Commonwealth), and of all countries covered by the Pan-American Copyright Convention, the Universal Copyright Convention, the Berne Convention, and of all countries with which the United States has reciprocal copyright relations. All rights, including professional/amateur stage rights, motion picture, recitation, lecturing, public reading, radio broadcasting, television, video or sound recording, all other forms of mechanical or electronic reproduction, such as CD-ROM, CD-I, DVD, information storage and retrieval systems and photocopying, and the rights of translation into foreign languages, are strictly reserved. Particular emphasis is placed upon the matter of readings, permission for which must be secured from the Author's agent in writing.

The stage performance rights in CAHOOTS (other than first class rights) are controlled exclusively by DRAMATISTS PLAY SERVICE, INC., 440 Park Avenue South, New York, NY 10016. No professional or non-professional performance of the Play (excluding first class professional performance) may be given without obtaining in advance the written permission of DRAMATISTS PLAY SERVICE, INC., and paying the requisite fee.

Inquiries concerning all other rights should be addressed to International Creative Management, Inc., 40 West 57th Street, New York, NY 10019. Attn: Mitch Douglas.

SPECIAL NOTE
Anyone receiving permission to produce CAHOOTS is required to give credit to the Author as sole and exclusive Author of the Play on the title page of all programs distributed in connection with performances of the Play and in all instances in which the title of the Play appears for purposes of advertising, publicizing or otherwise exploiting the Play and/or a production thereof. The name of the Author must appear on a separate line, in which no other name appears, immediately beneath the title and in size of type equal to 50% of the size of the largest, most prominent letter used for the title of the Play. No person, firm or entity may receive credit larger or more prominent than that accorded the Author.

CAHOOTS received its world premiere at The Mill Dinner Theatre at Sonning, England, in June, 1986. It was directed by David Taylor; the set and costume design was by Terry Parsons; the lighting design was by Steve Huttly. The cast was as follows:

JAN	Marlena Mackey
LOIS	Kate Harper
AL	Rolf Saxon
KEN	Jon Cartwright
GRANT	Douglas McFerran

CAHOOTS was produced in New York City by Gay Goldman, The Lerner-Rechnitz Group and Renee Blau at the South Street Theatre, where it opened March 4, 1990. It was directed by David Taylor; the set design was by Scott Bradley; the lighting design was by Malcolm Sturchio; the costume design was by Susan Young and the stage manager was Jessica Murrow. The cast was as follows:

JAN	Kathryn Meisle
LOIS	Katherine Leask
AL	Malachy Cleary
KEN	James DeMarse
GRANT	John Hickey

CHARACTERS

JAN — Actress in commercials, thirties
LOIS — Fiction editor, thirties
AL — Ad agency art director, thirties
KEN — Architect, thirties
GRANT — Uniformed officer, early twenties

SETTING
An apartment on the East Side of Manhattan.

ACT I
Scene 1: March. Early evening.
Scene 2: Ten minutes later.

ACT II
Ten minutes later.

CAHOOTS

ACT I

Scene 1

THE TIME: March, early evening.

THE PLACE: The living room of an apartment in midtown Manhattan.

AT RISE: It is nearly dark but enough light remains to see that the room is very well-furnished and has a number of framed architectural drawings on the walls. There are doors to the outside hall, a closet, and the kitchen, and a hall leading to the bedrooms. Several windows and a glass door, all without curtains, look out onto a terrace, where a shabbily-dressed man is in the process of breaking into the apartment. He slips the lock on the glass door, opens it and enters. A key turns in the lock of the outside hall door, then in a second lock, then in a third. The man looks around for a place to hide, opens the lid of a large antique chest, gets in, closes the lid. The door opens and two women enter, the first flicking a switch that turns on the lights. She is Jan Miller a pleasant-looking woman in her early thirties, well-dressed and carrying two shopping bags. Her companion, Lois Shields, is about the same age, and seems rather annoyed. She is wearing an old army coat and scuffed boots and carries a tote bag. Lois re-locks the three locks and fastens two chains on the door.

JAN. I'd better get this right in the oven.
LOIS. How much time do we have?
JAN. I told them we'd be there at seven.
LOIS. Do they know that means eight?
JAN. I said I'm sorry you had to wait in the lobby, Lois. You

know how auditions are. *(Jan puts one of the shopping bags on the couch, exits to the kitchen with the other.)*
LOIS. What can I do to help?
JAN. *(From kitchen.)* You could set the table while I start things in here. *(Lois goes to the antique chest, starts to open it. From kitchen.)* The linens are in the coat closet.
LOIS. Don't you always keep them in here?
JAN. *(From kitchen.)* Ken cleaned it out. He was going to refinish it Saturday. And the Saturday before that. *(Lois starts for the closet, passes Jan's shopping bag on the couch, can't resist looking inside.)*
LOIS. I see you found time to squeeze in a little shopping while I waited. *(Jan enters from the kitchen with china and silver just as Lois pulls a filmy black negligee out of the bag, then another in scarlet, with cutouts.)*
JAN. *(Embarrassed.)* I picked those up *before* the audition. *(Lois holds up a negligee.)*
LOIS. You're kidding.
JAN. I passed them in a store window and I couldn't resist.
LOIS. What store? Frederick's of Hollywood? *(She holds up another one, laughs.)*
JAN. What's so goddamn funny?
LOIS. You have to admit they're not exactly your style.
JAN. Maybe my style's changing. Besides, who are you to talk? You look more like a bag lady than a book editor.
LOIS. Do you love it? It's called "Dressing for Defense." The theory is that muggers take one look at you and decide you're not worth the effort. Must work. My throat wasn't cut once today.
JAN. Al?
LOIS. And the ongoing war against crime. You'll hear more about it later, complete with diagrams. *(Lois removes her boots, takes several pieces of jewelry and dress shoes from her tote bag, starts putting them on.)* So I guess we both dress to please our men. Those *are* for Ken, aren't they? *(Jan stuffs the lingerie in the chest, without looking inside.)*
JAN. He sleeps in his underwear.
LOIS. You know what I mean. Are you two having prob-

lems? Have the fires subsided?
JAN. What fires?
LOIS. Don't be so touchy. Come on, Jan, we've been friends a long time. Maybe I can help.
JAN. You want to help? Here. Put the cheese in the celery.
LOIS. You think you're the only woman in the world whose husband has that particular problem?
JAN. Well Al certainly — *(She stops herself.)*
LOIS. Al certainly what?
JAN. I mean he just doesn't seem the type.
LOIS. After twelve years of marriage, they're all the type. Make that three.
JAN. Have you tried to do anything about it?
LOIS. I've put Vitamin E on his Oat Bran.
JAN. Vitamin E on his Oat Bran?
LOIS. Yes. You crush the capsules and sprinkle it on. It's cheaper than X-rated lingerie and a lot more dignified.
JAN. Does it work?
LOIS. His cholesterol level I don't know about. His hormone level's still a problem, though. My problem. It doesn't seem to bother him.
JAN. I always thought you didn't care about sex.
LOIS. I don't. Unless he's having it with someone else.
JAN. Oh, Lois, Al's really not *that* type.
LOIS. They're all that type, too. After three *months* of marriage. Mmmm. What is that? Smells wonderful.
JAN. A cassoulet from some new place on Second Avenue. Midge Callender told me about it. *(Lois starts for the closet to get tablecloths and napkins. She glances out the window.)*
LOIS. Oh my God!
JAN. That's right. You haven't seen the new building.
LOIS. You've been Trumped!
JAN. It went up practically overnight. They ought to be renting it soon.
LOIS. You'll have to so something about these windows. For privacy. Drapes, maybe. Or those vertical blinds? At least they'll let in *some* light.
JAN. Who cares? I won't be here anyway. I'll be out

auditioning all day.
LOIS. How'd this one go today?
JAN. It was just for a commercial.
LOIS. What for?
JAN. McDonald's. They're opening them all over Eastern Europe.
LOIS. I guess they'll soon have all the blessings of democracy over there. I heard at the office today they're translating Judith Krantz into Polish. Did you get the part?
JAN. No. My hands were too big.
LOIS. What?
JAN. You see, what they do is, they cast normal-sized people with teeny-tiny hands so the Big Macs will look bigger.
LOIS. Can't win 'em all, I guess.
JAN. *You* seem to.
LOIS. You mean my million dollar career watching Arthur Weller drink lunch and then setting up the movie deals for those horror novels of his? That's not exactly my idea of winning.
JAN. But you *are* reasonably happy, aren't you? Despite your constant complaints.
LOIS. I'm reasonably content. I'm good at what I do. I make a good living.
JAN. Would you be more content without Al?
LOIS. Why this sudden concern for my marital happiness?
JAN. You're the one who brought it up.
LOIS. I did? Well, I don't want to talk about it anymore.
JAN. O.K. *(Jan crosses to bar and fixes drinks.)*
LOIS. Tell me about this thing tonight.
JAN. It'll be the four of us and the Murphys and the Carters. And the Seligs, of course. That's where they're holding it. Oh, and some cop from the Seventeenth Precinct.
LOIS. They've all been ripped off in the last year, right?
JAN. The cop I don't know about.
LOIS. Two kinds of wine, three kinds of cheese, and enough recent victims. The basic ingredients of an East Side block

association.
JAN. An awareness of crime is not paranoia.
LOIS. How about checking the closets every night when you get home?
JAN. Al does that?
LOIS. Also the shower enclosures. You never know where the Manson gang might be hiding. Tell me something. Why is Ken involved in this block association business? It can't be his comradely feelings for Al.
JAN. He wants to keep our neighborhood safe.
LOIS. Come on, Jan. He always looks bored to death when Al brings up crime. Not that everybody doesn't.
JAN. Al will get over his obsession. It's not even a year since his brother was killed.
LOIS. Do you realize *this* is our social life? We go to these anti-crime things liked my mother used to go to Tupperware parties. And that's it. When was the last time you had us over, for instance?
JAN. I don't remember off-hand.
LOIS. It's been two months.
JAN. Well, Ken's been working late and I've been out auditioning a lot.
LOIS. Oh, come off it. Why spend an evening with us when you can just rent *Death Wish?*
JAN. The last time he was here he was pretty well behaved.
LOIS. Hope springs eternal? Not if it's been married to Al for the last year, it doesn't. Come on, give. Why's Ken involved in this thing?
JAN. It's the Seligs. They're about to build a beach house in Bridgehampton.
LOIS. And he wants the commission!
JAN. He can practically taste it.
LOIS. Is there a lot of money involved?
JAN. Wait till you see the apartment. They're so rich they don't have to have antiques.
LOIS. I love it. Al thinks he's made a convert and instead he's being used as architect's bait.
JAN. The others are really interested.

LOIS. I knew it. He never could stand Al. God, remember the night we introduced them?
JAN. Who could forget? You never told him, did you? I think I would've told Ken. During a fight or something.
LOIS. Tell Al Ken thought he was gay? You must be kidding. We'd be seeing each other once a decade. *(The lid of the chest flies open, Al stands. He is in his forties, dressed rather shabbily, and very angry.)*
AL. *What!?!* *(Both women scream.)*
JAN and LOIS. AL!!
AL. He thought *I was what?!?*
JAN. Al!
LOIS. What are you doing here?
AL. He thought I was *what?!?*
LOIS. How did you get in?
AL. I slipped the lock with a credit card.
JAN. Which one?
AL. Bloomingdale's. He thought I was what?
JAN. No, I mean which lock. *(He points to the terrace door.)*
AL. That one.
JAN. But how'd you get out there?
AL. From the roof.
LOIS. Why, for God's sake?
AL. When I got here I saw you waiting in the lobby, so I thought I'd sneak up the service stairs and give everybody a little lesson about security. You think you're so safe? Well, here I am! I *could* be the Manson gang!
JAN. The roof!
LOIS. Oh, for God's sake, Al.
AL. *(To Lois.)* How come you never told me the son-of-a-bitch said that?
LOIS. It was just a remark he made the first time he met you. It's something anybody might say.
AL. What?!?
JAN. All he said was he thought you were a little old to have a roommate.
LOIS. And he only said that because your leg happened to brush his under the table.

AL. He thought I was making a pass at him? At him? *(To Jan.)* How come *you* never told me about any of this?
LOIS. Why should *she*?
JAN. Right. Why should I?
AL. My leg brushed his leg? What an egomaniac!
LOIS. Now, Al, try to calm down. We have to go to this meeting.
AL. So that no-talent creep can use me to get a goddamn commission?
LOIS. The others are sincere. Didn't you hear her say that?
AL. Yeah. I heard a lot of things in here. Vitamin E on my Oat Bran?
LOIS. Serves you right for spying.
JAN. Why didn't you come out earlier?
AL. I got interested. Besides, I was waiting for Ken to come. He's the one I wanted to make my point to. Until I heard what the son-of-a-bitch said!
LOIS. It was thirteen years ago.
JAN. We all know he was wrong now. Why let it upset your plans for the evening?
AL. You mean why let it interfere with my obsession. *(A key turns in the front door.)*
JAN. Oh, damn.
AL. Did you tell him Carl was my cousin and that I was only letting him share the apartment because my mother insisted?
JAN and LOIS. Yes. Yes! Yes! *(The other two locks unlock. The door opens, but not all the way, because of the chains.)*
KEN. *(From outside.)* Honey. *(Jan hurries to the door, shuts it, unlatches the chains. She and Ken have trouble trying to get all the locks unlocked simultaneously.)* Get away from the door! *(The door opens. Ken Miller enters, kisses her. He is a mild, pleasant-looking sort of man in his late forties. Jan re-locks the locks, puts on the chains.)* Hi, hon. Lois, Al. *(He notices that Al is standing in the open chest, glowering at him.)* Glad you could make it.
LOIS. Nice to see you again, Ken. How've you been?
KEN. Fine. How've you two been?
LOIS. Fine. Fine.

KEN. Good. Well, I really appreciate your coming tonight. The others do too. They'll tell you themselves later. It's nice to have friends who know so much about setting one of these things up.
JAN. How was your day? I found out my hands were too big and Lois drank lunch with Arthur Weller.
KEN. They're always reading his books at the office. The secretaries, I mean. Uh, Al, do you mind if I ask you something?
AL. Is it about my sex life?
KEN. What?
AL. Ask.
KEN. Why are you standing in my chest?
AL. I like to.
KEN. You like to?
AL. Yeah. Any objections? I mean, does that make me weird or anything? Does it make you suspicious?
KEN. No. It just struck me as odd.
AL. How was your day? Did you design anything wonderful? Like a beach house? Suitable for, say, Bridgehampton? *(Ken pours himself a drink.)*
KEN. I never design anything wonderful, not at the office. What we do there is, we keep taking this basic apartment and making everything six percent smaller every year. Bathrooms. Junior bedrooms. Faucets. Everything. I'm not an architect. I'm a miniaturizer. *(To Jan.)* Did it come?
JAN. What? Oh, yes. This afternoon. Just as I was running out to my audition. I haven't even had a chance to look at it myself. *(She gives him a large, flat package. He unwraps it, displays a framed architectural drawing. Al steps out of the chest.)*
LOIS. How nice. What is it?
AL. A set of ice cube trays with a matching ice bucket. Am I right?
JAN. It's a hospital.
KEN. A hospice.
JAN. For the fatally ill. With accommodations for their relatives.
AL. *(To Ken.)* That reminds me. My cousin Carl died. You

remember Carl. My mother forced me to share my apartment with him. Around the time we met.
KEN. Sorry to hear it. Now, the patients are over here on the right, the survivors-to-be on the left. Administration and medical facilities in the center block.
JAN. Including a Right to Die Suite. On the second floor here.
AL. Sort of the Final Marriott.
LOIS. It really is handsome. *(Al looks around the room at Ken's other drawings.)*
AL. Is that what keeps you going, Ken? Designing buildings that'll never be built?
KEN. Like Gandy. *(Jan exits to the kitchen.)*
LOIS. I didn't know he was an architect.
KEN. There was an earlier one who was. Gandy with a "y" but no "h."
AL. What?
KEN. G-A-N-D-Y. J.M. Gandy.
AL. Where and when didn't *his* buildings get built?
KEN. England. Early nineteenth century. He was a draftsman for a famous, very successful architect. They both died, and Gandy left behind the most amazing drawings. They were better than the master's.
LOIS. Which got built.
KEN. And later, destroyed. Most of them.
AL. But what's-his-name's live on. As yours will. Is that it?
KEN. I guess so.
AL. Have you ever considered doing something else, Ken?
KEN. You mean like running a little inn upstate or chartering fishing boats out of Falmouth? Of course. I'm no different than anybody else.
LOIS. Then why don't you?
KEN. I just told you. I'm no different than anybody else. *(To Al.)* What's yours?
AL. What's my what?
KEN. Your escape fantasy. And don't tell me you don't have one. You're no different than anybody else either.
LOIS. A book store.

KEN. Where?
LOIS. Albuquerque.
KEN. Why there?
LOIS. It's where the *Jane Fonda Workout* books do worst.
KEN. Nice climate. But a little short on advertising agencies, isn't it? *(To Al.)* What'll you do?
AL. I get to design bookmarks.
LOIS. It's a wonderful place. There are people there who still read books. Dense with text, very little white space, no pictures. While the rest of the reading public curls up with a copy of *How to Become a Real Person*.
KEN. Didn't your outfit publish that thing?
LOIS. It was our biggest seller last year. You wouldn't believe what it's done for my profit sharing! I keep wondering if there are that many people out there who consider themselves unreal. And think a book will help.
KEN. You won't move to Albuquerque.
LOIS. No. No. We won't. *(She looks at Ken's drawings.)* At least you have these. You've done what you like.
AL. Even if they will never be built. *(Jan returns from kitchen carrying a large wooden pepper mill.)*
JAN. Maybe you should get into editing novels that will never be published.
LOIS. I've tried that. Do you use that thing all the time or just when we come?
KEN. Just when you come.
AL. As a reminder of the good old days.
LOIS. *(To Al.)* I still can't believe you got it under your coat and out of the dining room without being stopped.
JAN. God, were you funny that night.
LOIS. Nobody else could've carried it off.
KEN. He had a lot of help from those drinks. The ones with the little blue umbrellas. What were they called?
AL. Frozen Belindas. Only the Casa Belvedere would have a drink called Belinda.
LOIS. And the decor. Cross-Bronx Expressway Elegante. In the middle of the Caribbean.
JAN. It was so awful. But we had a good time. We had a lot

of good times in those days. *(An uncomfortable pause.)*
KEN. Speaking of drinks, can I fix you one, Al? Scotch, isn't?
AL. Scotch will be fine. Make it a short one.
KEN. Want to keep your head for the meeting?
AL. When I drink too much, I lose all my sexual inhibitions.
KEN. Oh, really?
AL. Yeah. I wouldn't want to embarrass you by groping one of your straight friends.
KEN. What?
LOIS. I have a great idea. Why don't you give Ken and Jan a little preview of the Crimebusters presentation?
JAN. Terrific!
AL. They don't want to be subjected to the most boring man in America twice in one night.
JAN. Yes we do. I mean, we'd love to have a preview.
AL. *(To Ken.)* How about you, Ken?
KEN. Of course, Al. I'm very interested.
AL. Well, you should be. For all you know, the Manson gang's in the bedroom. *(Al goes out onto the terrace to get his presentation case.)*
KEN. Why is he...?
JAN. Don't ask. *(Al re-enters and opens presentation case on chest. He pulls out a flip chart, and assumes the air of a lecturer who has made his presentation many times. He points to the first card. It reads "CRIMEBUSTERS.")*
AL. "My friends, we are here this evening to put a stop to crime. What can we do, you might ask? As ordinary, law-abiding citizens, we..."
LOIS. *(Interrupts.)* Why don't you just give them some of the high points?
AL. It's all high points.
LOIS. They'll see the whole thing later. I know, do Defensive Walking.
KEN. What's Defensive Walking?
LOIS. It's like Defensive Dressing, only it's walking.
KEN. What's Defensive Dressing? *(Al flips the chart, passing cards labelled "Know Your Mugger," "Staying Alive on the A Train," "How Safe is Your Elevator?" and "Spotting Subway Shovers." He*

stops at one with the silhouette of a man walking labelled "Defensive Walking.")
AL. *(Pointing to his clothes.)* This is Defensive Dressing.
KEN. Oh, I get it. You look kind of seedy so you don't attract muggers, right?
AL. Right.
LOIS. Show him the walk. *(Al strides very purposefully and boldly across the room, shoulders back, eyes straight ahead.)*
KEN. That's it?
AL. That's Defensive Walking.
JAN. Very nice.
LOIS. The idea is not to look like a victim.
AL. You see, a lot of people actually invite muggers to attack them by walking in a passive, purposeless way.
KEN. So what are you inviting them to do? Pick you up?
AL. What?
JAN. Ken!
KEN. Don't you think it's a little heavy on the masculinity?
AL. You worry about that a lot, don't you, Ken? *(To Lois.)* I did not come here tonight to be heckled.
KEN. Sorry.
LOIS. Play the cassette for them.
AL. All right. *(Al takes a cassette from the presentation case.)*
LOIS. This was his idea. He had it made at the agency. *(Al flicks the switch. The sound of a dog barking is heard. Al flicks off the switch.)*
AL. That was me. Woof.
JAN. What a good idea.
AL. You just turn it on when you leave the apartment.
KEN. And it scares off burglars who are afraid of recorded dogs.
AL. Listen, Smart Ass, I've had about enough of your ...
KEN. Come on, Al. I'm just kidding. I'm sorry, I couldn't help myself. Why don't you relax and finish your drink? We'll see all this later and I promise to take it seriously. Here, let me hang up that jacket. *(He helps Al slip out of his jacket. As he does, a gun falls out of the pocket onto the coffee table.)*
JAN. Oh, Lord.

KEN. Oh, no. *(Al picks up the revolver. The others stare, horrified.)*
AL. No problem. Not even a dent.
KEN. You own a — a ...?
LOIS. I didn't know he had one.
AL. It's called a gun, folks.
KEN. You carry it around with you?
AL. Sure. It's smaller than an umbrella and a hell of a lot scarier.
LOIS. When did you get it?
AL. Last week.
LOIS. You mean that's been in the apartment for a week? *(He nods.)* I didn't even know you had a permit.
AL. I don't.
KEN. You mean you're carrying it around illegally?
AL. So I'm a criminal. Terrific. Puts me on the winning side for a change.
KEN. And you brought that thing into my home?
AL. I don't intend to shoot anybody. Not even you.
KEN. Of course you don't intend to harm anybody. But having one of those things around ... well, somebody could get hurt.
AL. First of all, it's a gun. Just one syllable. Screw up your manly courage. I'm sure you can say it.
KEN. Listen, Al, if you want to break the law somewhere else by carrying a concealed weapon, fine. But not in my home.
AL. It's not concealed anymore.
JAN. Please put it away. It makes me nervous. *(Al returns the gun to his pocket.)*
AL. You're safe now. Although it is concealed again. But you know it's there, so technically you're okay.
KEN. Does anybody need a ...? *(Ken, Jan and Lois hurry to the bar.)*
AL. Why are you all staring at me like that? I just want to stay alive. It's not an unreasonable goal. If I were, say, the convicted murderer of five or six old ladies and the state wanted to kill me, you'd be organizing a protest rally to save

my life. But because I want to do it myself, you're horrified.
LOIS.   How did you get a ... gun?
AL.   It's easy for us criminals. You law-abiding citizens are the ones who have problems getting guns. Can't have the victims walking around armed. *(He sniffs.)* Is that an electrocution I smell? If so, it's about time.
JAN.   Oh, damn. The cassoulet. *(Jan exits to kitchen.)*
LOIS.   If it's ruined, we can always send the Terminator out for another one.
JAN.   *(From kitchen.)* It's salvageable. But we'll have to eat right away. *(Lois exists to kitchen.)*
KEN.   Another drink?
AL.   I already told you. I know my limit. *(Al sits in the arm chair and Ken sits on the couch, as far away as possible. Long pause.)* Ever notice how the minutes fly like hours when we're together?
KEN.   Jesus, Al, a gun. *(Jan enters, puts fruit cups on the table.)*
AL.   You been down to the morgue lately, Ken? *(Jan laughs nervously, exits to kitchen.)*
KEN.   And without a permit. Some Crimebuster.
AL.   I asked if you'd been down to the morgue lately.
KEN.   No, I haven't.
AL.   You should go. It's a little out of the way, but you'd like the crowd. Your kind of people. All in drawers. The kind you pull out.
KEN.   I'd rather not discuss it.
AL.   Could be your future I'm talking about. Not very open of you not to want to discuss the future.
KEN.   Okay. Okay. I'll talk about it. Tell me this. What put those people in those drawers?
AL.   Other people, mostly.
KEN.   But what did they use as weapons? I've got you on this one, pal, statistically.
AL.   You've got me on what? That some of the people in the drawers were killed by guns? The ones that weren't stabbed. So what? The point is that it's not the people on file who had the guns. And used them. It's the people that are still out there, walking the streets.

KEN. There's just no point in arguing with you people, is there?
AL. You People! I'll bet you knew all along I'd turn into You People.
KEN. For once in your life, you're right. I never did like you.
AL. I was never sure why exactly. Was it because I was in advertising or because I walked funny? *(Lois enters with wine bottle and glasses, puts them on the dining table.)*
LOIS. What's the matter?
AL. Nothing's the matter. Old Ken and I were just discussing why he never liked me.
LOIS. Oh, Al, please.
AL. What could be more pleasant than a nice, open, honest guy like Ken being nice and open and honest?
LOIS. Stop it. You've been nasty enough for one night.
AL. Let me see. If it wasn't my girlish walk and it wasn't my line of work, what could it have been?
LOIS. Al, I'm warning you. *(Jan enters with cassoulet.)*
JAN. What's the matter?
AL. Your beloved husband won't tell me why he hated me on sight. I got it! It was Saint Paul's Cathedral, wasn't it? *(To Lois.)* Remember? That first night we met. I said I liked it and he damned near threw up in his pasta primavera. As a matter of fact, I think he said something about the dome being slightly out of scale before he went into his sulk. Am I right?
JAN. Ken. Please.
KEN. Goddamit, I...
JAN. Please.
KEN. *(To Al.)* Okay! You're right!
JAN. Now let's have our dinner. *(They sit.)*
AL. You're goddamn right I'm right.
LOIS. And Midge Callender was right too. This looks delicious.
JAN. Wait till dessert. I couldn't choose between the lemon tarts and the sacher torte.
AL. *(To Ken.)* I'm right about everything, including the gun.
LOIS. *(To Jan.)* Which did you choose, finally?

KEN. *(To Al.)* That I can't agree with.
JAN. *(To Lois.)* The Black Forest cake. They do it with brandied cherries and very dark chocolate cake and the whole thing is ...
AL. *(To Ken.)* Yeah? You could if it was *your* brother they found next to the morning's garbage with a hole that big in him.
JAN. *(To Lois.)* ... covered with whipped cream and slivered almonds.
KEN. I'm sorry your brother is dead, Al. You have my sympathy. But not the right to torture me.
LOIS. He's right. A lot of people lose people that way these days and they don't turn into Genghis Khan over it.
JAN. Try the butter. It's from Normandy.
AL. People get mugged. Sometimes they get killed in the process. Is that what you mean?
LOIS. *(To Jan.)* Normandy? Oh, all those sweet little stone farm houses.
KEN. *(To Al.)* Unfortunately, it's part of urban living.
JAN. *(To Lois.)* And it tastes like it came from Normandy.
AL. *(To Ken.)* Like dog shit. It's there, but if you don't look at it and you don't step in it, it won't affect you.
LOIS. *(To Jan.)* Mmmmm. It does.
KEN. *(To Al.)* In a way, yes.
AL. Well, haven't you noticed that if you don't look at it, you have a hell of a hard time not stepping in it? That's what happened to Jerry. He was crazy! Just like all of you are.
JAN. Try one of these rolls, Al.
LOIS. Where are they from?
JAN. Pepperidge Farm.
KEN. It's been eleven months since your brother's death. Look, Al, as long as you brought up the subject, I'm going to say something that should've been said months ago. You should be in therapy.
AL. Makes sense. The streets are full of criminals and crazies. I'm alarmed by it, so I should be in therapy.
LOIS. He's right, Al.

AL. That's two out of three. And this *is* a democracy. Dog-shit-ridden, but still a democracy. Tell you what. Right after this meeting you're having to prevent what I'm imagining, I'll hurry down to Bellevue and turn myself in. Shouldn't be difficult. Most of our mental institutions are empty. You know what they give them when they turn them loose? A shopping bag full of drugs and a butcher knife. They can use whichever they like. Freedom of choice!
KEN. Nobody said anything about Bellevue.
AL. Okay. Some good private hundred-dollar an hour shrink then. What'll I tell him? That I'm paranoid? That I think a lot of people out there want to kill me? They do! You're the ones who are crazy.
LOIS. Now, Al, calm down. This is getting out of hand.
JAN. I have some of their paté in the fridge. Would anybody...
AL. *(To Lois.)* You. You're not just crazy. You're a hypocrite. We've got more locks and chains in that apartment than *these* maniacs do. And this is practically the Tower of London. You put them there. You stopped getting the Sunday *Times* on a Saturday night because you're afraid to go down to the corner after dark. And you hate your stupid job and walking through garbage and danger and madmen to get to it. But you won't leave this place and go somewhere else — somewhere safe, somewhere civilized.
JAN. You asked her to?
AL. No, but she wouldn't anyway. She loves New York.
KEN. And you hate it. If you feel so strongly, why don't you leave?
AL. You think I hate this town? I love this town! That's why I feel this way!
KEN. That alone should keep his therapist busy for weeks.
AL. Oh yeah? You know something? You're the craziest of all. You take the subway to work. At least she has enough sense left to walk the twenty blocks so she'll be able to run a few yards when they come after her. You'll probably just be sitting there, smiling your smug little smile, thinking about world peace when they blow you away. No! I know

what you'll be doing. You'll be designing one of your stupid imaginary buildings.
LOIS.   Now that *is* enough.
KEN.   No. Let him finish.
AL.   *(To Jan.)* You know what really got to me when they killed Jerry? It was at the funeral home. *(He indicates Ken.)* This asshole came up to me and clutched me. At first I thought he was going to tell me there was a bright side to murder. But I was wrong. You know what he wanted? He wanted to design a fucking headstone for my brother. *(To Ken.)* For all I know, you did one and it's out for framing. And it probably stinks, like all the rest of this crap you've got hanging on the walls. You know something — Marcel Breuer or Mies Van der Roe or whoever it is you think you are? The reason your buildings aren't built isn't because today's architecture is second-rate. It's because *you* are. No, that's too generous. You're fifth-rate!
KEN.   Yeah? What about you? All the bullshit I've been listening to for twelve years about what a fabulous artist you are and how you're forced to work in an advertising agency until that glorious day when you've got enough money to chuck it all and do the kind of thing you're really capable of. Well, you know what you're really capable of? Exactly what you're doing. Detergent boxes. Cat food cans. Condom display racks!
JAN.   Okay, guys, this has gone far enough.
AL.   At least I can get work without pretending to be a public-spirited citizen to get a job.
KEN.   What?
LOIS.   *(To Ken.)* Ignore him. He doesn't really mean any of this.
JAN.   Please, Al.
AL.   I heard all about it when I was in the trunk. You learn a lot in trunks.
KEN.   What?
JAN.   Al, for God's sake, will you get control of yourself.
AL.   You don't give a damn *how* much violence there is in this town! You don't care if it turns into one continuous

murder spree as long as you get yours!
LOIS. He does. That's why we're here tonight.
KEN. You're crazy. I'm just as much against violence as you are.
AL. Hah.
JAN. He's against it. He just said so.
KEN. I am!
LOIS. See?
AL. The hell you are. All you care about is yourself.
KEN. Listen. If I say I'm sincerely against violence, I'm sincerely against violence.
AL. Hah!
KEN. I am against violence.
AL. Hah — *hah!*
KEN. I am, goddamit. I am.
AL. Hah-hah-*hah!*
KEN. I'm against violence, you son-of-a-bitch! I'm against violence. I'm against it! I'm... (*In a flash, Ken grabs the pepper mill and swings it at Al, striking him on the temple. The women scream.*)

CURTAIN

Scene 2

THE TIME: Ten minutes later.

THE PLACE: The same.

AT RISE: Al is still seated at the table. He is in exactly the same position as before. A pink linen napkin, spotted with blood, covers his face. Ken, who is coming out of shock but heading for panic, sits on the sofa. He rises, crosses to the bar, avoids looking at Al, and pours himself a large Scotch, then goes to the bedroom hall.

KEN. Jan! Jan!
JAN. (*From bedroom.*) Just a minute, dear. (*He crosses behind*

the couch, still careful not to look at Al. Jan enters, looks at Al.) You put that on him?
KEN.   He certainly didn't. I couldn't take the stare.
JAN.   Pink?
KEN.   You don't think the color's appropriate? How is she?
JAN.   I gave her some Valium. She's settling down. It's got blood on it.
KEN.   You want to change his napkin?
JAN.   Of course not. We're not supposed to touch anything until the police get here. You know that. Make me one of those. Straight. *(She sits down, stares at Al. Ken brings her a drink.)* I can't believe he's dead. Good God. It's getting bigger.
KEN.   What is?!?
JAN.   The blood stain. *(A pause.)* Actually, it isn't a blood stain. Yet. It's still just blood.
KEN.   Will you for Christ's sake stop talking about it?
JAN.   What would you like me to talk about? The stock market? You just murdered our best friend in cold blood.
KEN.   He was not my best friend. And my blood was anything but cold!
JAN.   All right. The husband of *my* best friend.
KEN.   You couldn't stand him either. You said so yourself last night.
JAN.   You said so. I merely agreed with you.
KEN.   You didn't have to.
JAN.   No? Look what happens to people who don't! Poor Al.
KEN.   Don't be a hypocrite. Don't pretend you liked him now that he's — gone.
JAN.   That's your justification, I suppose. He wasn't likeable. And, of course, if someone isn't likeable, you have him over for dinner and bash his head in. Happens all the time.
KEN.   He moved. That's what did it. If he hadn't, it wouldn't have hit him on the temple. The bone is sort of thin there. If it had struck him higher, he'd probably just have a fractured skull. A concussion, even.
JAN.   So, in a way, it was his own fault. Is that what you're

saying?
KEN.   I'm saying he moved and that made it worse.
JAN.   People have a tendency to move when attacked with a three foot pepper mill!
KEN.   Calm down.
JAN.   This isn't happening. That's it. It isn't happening. I'm asleep or I'm hallucinating or something. *(She shuts her eyes tightly, then opens them.)* You never did anything like this before in your life. With his own pepper mill. How could you?
KEN.   Damned if I know. It just happened. I felt like I was watching somebody else do it.
JAN.   What's taking them so long? I want to get it over with. I'd ... I'd like him out of here.
KEN.   Us out of here!
JAN.   Us?
KEN.   Us. Him — and me. The victim goes to the morgue. The murderer goes to jail.
JAN.   Don't call yourself that.
KEN.   That's what I am. *(A silence.)*
JAN.   Jail?
KEN.   Directly. Do not pass go, do not collect two hundred dollars.
JAN.   But you'll be out in the morning?
KEN.   Sure. For a while.
JAN.   Oh, come on. You won't be ... sentenced, or anything like that. I mean, it was practically an accident. He moved.
KEN.   No, it was a crime. Of passion. But nevertheless a crime. When one man strikes another man with a pepper mill and the second man dies from it, it's a crime. No matter *what* the son-of-a-bitch said.
JAN.   I couldn't believe he said that. I didn't think he could *be* that vicious. To attack you on ... Wait a minute! You'll get off! Because of what he said. There's some legal term for it. Undue something or other. We can all testify to it. Even Lois will, I'm sure. She's a little angry right now, but she's basically an honest person.
KEN.   So we hire a lawyer and he tells a jury that I killed Al

because he criticized my drawings. And they say, "Oh, did he really? Well, in that case, he deserved to die." No, we'd better face it. I'm going to do time.
JAN. You, in jail?
KEN. Yes. For ten years, probably.
JAN. My God, what'll I do?
KEN. What'll *you* do? I'm the one who's going to jail!
JAN. And I'm the one who has to keep things together so you'll have someplace to come home to when you get out!
KEN. You're right. I completely forgot the position this puts you in. At least I'll have a roof over my head and something to eat.
JAN. Something to — What have we got? In the bank, I mean.
KEN. About forty thousand dollars.
JAN. That's all? Forty thousand? Didn't we have ...?
KEN. We used it for the down payment on the beach house.
JAN. But won't the company ...?
KEN. They'll wash their hands of me so fast your head'll spin.
JAN. It already is. Do you know what forty thousand is divided by ten years? Four thousand a year. I couldn't even pay the rent. You know what I made last year.
KEN. I suppose you could give up this place and live at the beach.
JAN. But I couldn't *work* out there. And the mortgage there is more than the rent here. What am I going to do? Doesn't your insurance cover situations like this?
KEN. You'll be eligible for welfare.
JAN. Welfare?
KEN. But I think they'll make you sell the car.
JAN. *(Panicked.)* Good God, what are we going to do? You've committed a crime and the police are going to be here any second and — Oh, Ken, what are we going to do?
KEN. What did you tell them exactly?
JAN. What did I tell who?
KEN. The police.
JAN. The police? I didn't call the police. You mean you

didn't call the police?
KEN. No. I thought you called them from in there.
JAN. I was taking care of Lois. I thought you called them from out here.
KEN. The witness is the one who calls the police! Not the mur — not the perpetrator.
JAN. Excuse me. I'm new at this.
KEN. Maybe this is a blessing in disguise. It gives us time to think.
JAN. Think?
KEN. Yes. Let's try to calm down and evaluate the situation and then decide what action to take.
JAN. When something like this happens in your apartment you call the police. Right away. That is the action you take. Or it's another crime. *(She goes to the phone.)*
KEN. If it's murder. This is beginning to look more like an accident. You said so yourself.
JAN. That's true.
KEN. An accident that's already claimed one victim. Should we let it claim two more? Would my going to jail and you starving bring Al back?
JAN. No. *(She hangs up the phone.)*
KEN. It's funny. This whole business has shown me how right Al was about things.
JAN. He said it was dangerous here. He sure was right about that.
KEN. And he was right about this society. What did he say — it isn't civilized here, it isn't safe? That's certainly true about the criminal justice system. And I would've been at the mercy of it.
JAN. But what do we do about — ? *(She indicates Al.)*
KEN. The first problem is Lois. She's a witness.
JAN. You don't mean ... ?
KEN. For God's sake, what do you think I am? What I mean is, we have to get her on our side in this thing.
JAN. Good luck. You just killed her husband. People are touchy about things like that.
KEN. How much Valium did you give her?

JAN. Five milligrams. No, I think it was ten. Are the yellow ones five and the white ten? Or are the blue — ?
KEN. *(Interrupts.)* Bring her out here. Maybe we can reason with her. *(She starts toward the bedroom, stops, goes to a cabinet, replaces Al's pink napkin with a fresh white one.)*
JAN. There, he's a little more presentable. *(A pause.)* He said some horrible things to you. *(She exits. Ken pours a cup of coffee. Jan returns with Lois. She looks at Al, screams.)*
KEN. Sit her down on the couch. *(Jan guides Lois to the couch. Ken approaches, holding out the coffee.)*
LOIS. Don't come near me!
KEN. Drink this. It'll make you feel better. *(He gives the drink to Jan, who hands it to Lois.)*
LOIS. Did you make this, Murderer? *(He nods, she pointedly puts it on the coffee table.)*
KEN. Let's try to keep our heads. We're all in shock. There's been a terrible accident.
LOIS. Accident? You call murdering Al with a pepper mill an accident? Murderer!
KEN. Okay, okay. There's been a terrible ... occurrence here and we have to discuss it like rational human beings.
LOIS. You want to discuss my husband's murder like rational human beings. *(To Jan.)* Is he crazy?
JAN. No, Lois, he's not. We're just all very, very upset.
LOIS. But he sounds like he wants to have a seminar or something.
KEN. I think it would be helpful to all concerned if we kept our voices down a bit.
LOIS. *(Screaming.)* The Pepper Mill Killer wants us to keep our voices down! Is that why you did it, Pepper Mill Killer, because Al's voice was too loud? Is that why you committed murder!?!
JAN. You *are* just a little loud, if you don't mind my saying so. *(To Ken.)* And this is with all the Valium.
KEN. Drink your coffee, Lois. *(To Jan.)* Thank God the walls are thick.
LOIS. Why are we talking about walls? And coffee? *(To Jan.)* You're crazy, too! Wait a minute. Why aren't the cops

here? *(She looks at her watch.)* It must be half an hour.
KEN. That's one of the things we'd like to discuss. But first, let me say, from the bottom of my heart, that I am very, very sorry for what happened here tonight.
LOIS. You haven't called the police!
KEN. Truly sorry.
LOIS. You haven't, have you?
KEN. No. No, we haven't. Not yet.
LOIS. Why not?
KEN. Well, we wanted to have this little talk first.
LOIS. We? *(To Jan.)* Are you in on this?
KEN. You see, it concerns her most of all.
LOIS. My husband is sitting there dead and we're going to have a discussion about *her*. What is this, Est?
KEN. Look, Lois. Jan is your best friend, isn't she?
LOIS. You want to discuss friendship? *(To Jan.)* The Pepper Mill Killer wants to discuss friendship!
KEN. But she *is* your best friend? You admit that?
LOIS. Yes, goddamit. But I don't see what that has to do with anything!
KEN. It has everything to do with — what happened. You see, Jan is the one who stands to be the most damaged by it. Next to Al, of course.
LOIS. *(To Jan.)* What is he talking about?
JAN. I've only got forty thousand dollars, Lois. That's all I've got. Forty thousand dollars.
LOIS. *(To Ken.)* What is she talking about?
KEN. She means to live on. If I go to jail.
LOIS. You just turned me into a widow and you want to discuss *her* financial problems?
JAN. You'll get Al's insurance money. All I've got is forty thousand dollars.
LOIS. I wish you'd stop saying that. You sound like you're applying for a loan or something. *(To Ken.)* What do you mean, *if* you go to jail?
KEN. What I mean is that if we call the police, and if I'm arrested and tried and convicted and sentenced, Jan here — who you have just admitted is your best friend — will

probably starve to death. Well, maybe not starve to death. But she'll have a very tough time. *(Lois rises, goes to the phone, dials three digits.)*
LOIS. At the moment, I don't care if she dies the death of a thousand cuts. I just want the cops here. You people are crazy. It is 9-1-1, isn't it? For an emergency? *(Jan crosses to table, picks up pepper mill, wipes it clean with napkin. Ken sees Jan and crosses to Lois.)* I've heard it takes a long time, but this is ridiculous. *(Jan hands the pepper mill to Lois as Ken takes the phone from her. Lois absent-mindedly accepts pepper mill, then realizes what's happened.)* Why did you put this — thing in my hand?
JAN. *(Crying.)* I'm sorry, Lois.
KEN. So your fingerprints will be on it. *(To Jan.)* Thanks, honey. *(Ken throws a kiss to Jan as he hangs up the phone.)*
JAN. *(Crying.)* I'm sorry. I'm sorry.
LOIS. My fingerprints? *(Lois drops the pepper mill on the couch.)*
KEN. Now when we tell the police that you killed Al, only your prints will be on the weapon.
LOIS. But you did it. You — I saw you pick it up. Yours are on it too.
JAN. *(Crying.)* I wiped it clean while you were dialing. I'm sorry, Lois.
LOIS. This is ridiculous. Why would I kill my own husband?
JAN. Why would she kill her own husband? *(Pause.)*
KEN. You found out he was having an affair.
LOIS. Oh, for God's sake, who would have an affair with Al?
KEN. Jan would!
JAN. I would?
KEN. Don't you remember? It was right after I told her you and Al were cheating on her and me that she went for the pepper mill.
JAN. Oh.
KEN. Then you tried to stop her. But she was too fast for you.
JAN. I remember now. *(Lois staggers to the couch, collapses, sobbing.)*

KEN. Of course you do. Just like you remember confessing to me last night. You told me all about it, right down to the smallest detail. How many times you did it, where...
JAN. *(Interrupts.)* I said I remember! I mean, that's enough. Can't you see she's out of her mind? *(She goes to Lois.)*
LOIS. Don't you come near me, you madwoman! You're worse than he is. At least he did what he did in the heat of an argument. You're doing this for money. But then, you always were a whore.
JAN. Let's not say anything we'll be sorry for later.
LOIS. *(To Ken.)* How do you think she got all those parts she bombed in when she first came to New York? On her back, that's how. She started with stage managers and worked her way up. I was her roommate. I used to hear her auditioning all night in the living room.
JAN. Lois!
LOIS. *(To Ken.)* But you don't have to worry. Obviously, nobody's interested in the merchandise these days. She can't even get a hamburger commercial. *(To Jan.)* And you call yourself an actress. You got one good notice — in a musical — and they were reviewing your tits!
JAN. At least I had tits worth reviewing.
LOIS. Had is right!
JAN. It's too bad you didn't go on the stage. You're quite an actress, you are. *(To Ken.)* Less than an hour ago she was telling me how she couldn't wait to be rid of Al.
LOIS. I never said I wanted to be rid of him. I said he was boring. You said *he* couldn't get it up. Does that mean you want to be rid of him?
KEN. What?
LOIS. Oh, go eat your Oat Bran! *(She looks at Al, starts sobbing again.)* He was just starting to come out of it, and you killed him.
JAN. You call that coming out of it? Carrying a gun? Viciously attacking the only friends he had left? *(Lois has picked up Al's jacket, clutches it to her bosom.)*
LOIS. Some friends! He was improving. There were signs. Signs that only a wife could see.

KEN. Be careful. The gun's still in the pocket. It could go off. *(Lois notices something in the other pocket, pulls out a thick wad of folded paper.)*
LOIS. What's all this? *(She unfolds it, reads the first paper.)* My God. He left the agency. Today was his last day. *(She goes to the next sheet.)* He got all his profit sharing. Here's the — it's a cashier's check. *(Ken reads the amount.)*
KEN. You *are* in good shape. What's that?
LOIS. His insurance policy. It says it's in force for thirty days after his — termination.
JAN. Two hundred and eighty thousand! And you want to condemn *me* to a life of poverty! *(Lois finds more checks.)*
LOIS. And he cleaned out the money market fund. And the savings account.
KEN. Cashier's checks?
LOIS. Yes.
KEN. I thought so. What's that little slip of paper?
LOIS. It's Al's writing, but I don't know what it means. *(Reads.)* "P.A. 304, 9734000." What can that mean?
KEN. The last part could be a phone number.
JAN. Isn't it too long?
LOIS. No, he's right. 973-4000.
KEN. What's before that?
LOIS. P.A. 304
JAN. Maybe it's the area code.
LOIS. But what's P.A.?
JAN. Pennsylvania?
KEN. Or Pan American! Yeah, it makes sense. He quits his job, cashes in all his chips — in checks that are negotiable anywhere. I'll bet you any one of them P.A. 304 is a flight number. And the phone number's for Pan American Airlines.
LOIS. But he wasn't planning a trip. I'd have known.
KEN. He said he wanted to get out of New York.
LOIS. He also said he wanted me to go with him.
JAN. What he said was that he wouldn't even bother to ask.
LOIS. He *was* going to ask. I'm sure of it. When we got home. Al wouldn't do a thing like this.

KEN. There's a way to find out.
LOIS and JAN. How?
KEN. Call the number. See if it's Pan Am and if they have a flight 304, and ask if you have a reservation. *(Jan starts for the phone.)* No, she should hear it herself. *(Lois goes to the phone, dials. There is a pause.)* Is it Pan Am?
LOIS. It's Liza Minnelli, singing "New York, New York."
JAN and KEN. It's Pan Am. *(They wait.)*
LOIS. Hello, Pan Am? *(A beat.)* Do you have a Flight Number 304? *(A beat.)* What is its destination? *(A pause.)* On tomorrow's flight, do you have a reservation for Mr. Alfred Shields? *(A pause.)* Is there one for Mrs. Shields? *(A beat.)* Are you absolutely sure of that? *(A beat.)* Thank you. *(She hangs up, turns toward Al.)* You son-of-a-bitch! *(She moves toward him.)* You rotten, crummy thief. That was *our* money. Half of it was mine. Hell, more than half. *(To Jan.)* I made more than he did, a lot more. The lousy egomaniac made me promise I'd never tell anybody. *(To Al.)* You were a creep, Al! A miserable, double-crossing, thieving creep. She was right. I couldn't wait to get rid of you. The Pepper Mill Killer did me a favor.
KEN. Where was he going?
LOIS. Rio. With my money! New York's top Crimebuster, and all the time he was planning to rip me off!
KEN. Calm down. We have to make plans.
LOIS. We?
JAN. You're in this now, too.
LOIS. If you're referring to that crap about your alleged affair with Al, forget it. Even Al could've done better. Besides, he was beating it for Rio.
JAN. That's not a bad motive either. Let's just say you found all this stuff out *before* you went for the pepper mill.
LOIS. Blackmail! Let's see, so far you've covered murder, failure to report a crime, and tampering with evidence. What's next, arson?
KEN. She's got another reason to join us. *(He gives her Al's insurance policy.)* See paragraph 8, section C. It's called double indemnity.

LOIS. As in Barbara Stanwyck?
KEN. I've always suspected people have made a lot more than a movie out of it. Do you realize how many accidental deaths happen every year? And how many heirs get twice the amount of insurance?
LOIS. Twice?
KEN. Five hundred and sixty instead of two hundred and eighty. If we convince the cops it was an accident.
JAN. You're practically a millionaire.
LOIS. You really think I'll go along with this?
KEN. Look, Lois, Al's gone. Will my going to jail or you losing your job bring him back?
LOIS. Losing my job? How would I lose my job?
KEN. How long would they keep an accused murderess on staff?
LOIS. You did it. I'll just tell the truth.
JAN. You accuse him. We accuse you. Two against one.
KEN. And then the whole mess hits the front page of the *Daily News.* "Horror Editor Slays Mate!"
JAN. "In Posh East Side Sex Triangle."
KEN. You choice, Lois. *(A brief pause.)*
LOIS. So what do we tell the cops? The pepper mill fell on him?
JAN. What if he went into the bathroom and slipped? Don't most accidents in the home happen that way?
KEN. That's in the shower. Why would he take a shower here?
JAN. Right. Why would he?
LOIS. It's too bad you didn't ask him to step outside for your brawl.
JAN. Oh, yes. Then he could've accidentally gone over the side in the scuffle. That's good, Lois.
KEN. That's it! That's it! Only without the scuffle.
LOIS. What are you talking about?
KEN. Now the thing is to stay as close to the truth as possible. It's easier to lie that way.
JAN. The truth?
KEN. There was an argument and he went out on the ter-

race to cool off. Alone. And then ... *(He makes a diving gesture.)*
LOIS. But how did he...? *(She imitates diving gesture.)*
KEN. We don't know.
JAN. We don't know?
KEN. When they come running up with the news, the three of us will be at the table, waiting for his return.
JAN. You mean you're actually going to ...? *(She makes a throwing gesture.)*
KEN. No, I mean *we're* going to. *(He grabs Al under the armpits.)*
JAN. Can't we — hide him somewhere?
KEN. He can't just disappear.
LOIS. Why not?
KEN. For one thing, you'd have to wait seven years to collect.
LOIS. Oh. *(She takes a leg.)*
JAN. Seven years isn't so long. You make a good living.
KEN. You don't. Remember? Welfare. Starvation. No car! *(She takes a leg.)*
JAN. I can't touch him. *(Jan and Lois each drop their legs, back off.)*
KEN. Lois?
LOIS. He was *my* husband.
KEN. And you're his beneficiary.
LOIS. I can't.
KEN. This is the double indemnity part.
LOIS. I still can't.
KEN. No more movie deals, Lois. No more power lunches. *(She takes a leg. To Jan.)* Welfare. Starvation. No car. *(She takes a leg. They start for the terrace.)*
JAN. Hold everything. What about Rio? *(Ken leaves the women each holding a leg, goes to the couch, takes the slip of paper with the flight number on it, tears it up, stuffs the pieces down the front of his trousers.)*
KEN. This about Rio.
LOIS. But what if they check?
JAN. Why would they? But what about the gun?

LOIS. It just helps prove what kind of shape he was in. *(They start to carry Al onto the terrace.)*
KEN. I completely forgot the damn thing was there. I feel better. We'll never know for sure, of course, but maybe what I did tonight was saving a life. Lives, even.
JAN. Yeah?
LOIS. *(To Jan.)* Maybe he's right. He had that thing in the apartment for a week and never told me.
KEN. For all we know, it was going to be Goodbye, Lois in more ways than one.
LOIS. My God.
JAN. He *was* crazed. I never saw anybody that crazed.
LOIS. He just got worse and worse as the months went by.
KEN. He was in terrible pain, poor guy. Well, he's out of his misery now. I ... well, I guess you could almost say it was a mercy killing.
LOIS. You could.
JAN. Maybe that's why he moved. Maybe he wanted it to — end. *(They throw Al off the terrace.)*

CURTAIN

END OF ACT I

ACT II

THE TIME: Ten minutes later.

THE PLACE: The same.

AT RISE: Jan, Lois and Ken are seated in silence at the table. Mozart is on the radio. There is a lot of tension.

KEN. This is no good. Look, it's very important that we act normally, so that when the police get here we'll seem ... normal.
LOIS. How in God's name do we do that?
KEN. We just do it. Now.
JAN. Now?
KEN. Yes. We're having an ordinary conversation. Al is out on the terrace.
JAN. Where do we start?
KEN. Wherever you like. Just start. *(A pause.)*
JAN. So, there I was, squashed into a corner. And he's licking my shopping bag, trying to get at the groceries.
KEN. Good. At least he wasn't trying to make love to your leg. That's what he always does to me.
JAN. I think it's unfair to have a dog in the city, especially a big one. Don't you, Lois? *(A pause. They look at Lois, who does not respond.)*
KEN. You should see him. He takes up half our elevator.
JAN. On the other hand, what's-her-name — the woman who owns him — seems to be crazy about him.
KEN. Ellis. I think her name is Ellis.
JAN. Yes. That's it. Ellis.
KEN. Right. Her last name is Ellis. And the dog? What's the dog's name?
JAN. Gordon. At least that's what she always says at the butcher shop, "I mustn't forget Gordon's chopped sirloin."
KEN. And the coat!
JAN. *(To Lois.)* He has this coat for his winter walks. Alpaca, Lois. *(A pause. They look at Lois.)*

37

LOIS. I can't do this anymore. *(She rises, turns off the radio.)*
KEN. Come on, Lois. You want everything to go right when they get here, don't you? We have to create the mood.
LOIS. I don't care. I cannot simulate a dinner party for one more minute.
JAN. I can't either. I'm sorry, I just can't.
KEN. All right, if you two aren't willing to do what's necessary, we're in a lot of trouble. Big trouble, Jan. Come on, we're having an ordinary conversation.
JAN. So many people in this building are strange about pets.
KEN. Thanks, honey.
LOIS. Looks who's so calm and reasonable all of a sudden.
KEN. Like the Cat Man.
LOIS. Nothing to worry about with our Ken in charge. Unless there's a blunt instrument within reach.
JAN. He's this older man on nine with — oh, he must have a dozen cats.
KEN. That's why we call him the Cat Man.
LOIS. You're really running things aren't you? All those years as an architect, wasted. What you should have been was a criminal.
JAN. The funny thing is he always wears navy.
KEN. Winter and summer.
LOIS. You're one of those people who discovers his true vocation a little late in life. Pity for Al it wasn't weaving.
KEN. Let's not start bickering, Lois.
JAN. Navy cardigans. Navy suits. He even has a pea coat.
KEN. *(To Lois.)* Sometimes in an emergency, when a leader's required, a leader emerges.
JAN. And they're always covered with cat hair.
LOIS. I give up. I *have* to see what's happing down there. *(Lois starts for the terrace.)*
KEN. No! *(Ken reaches out and grabs her by her dress. It tears.)*
JAN. Naturally, he likes white cats. Or gray. There's even an orange one. Her name is Betsy, I think.
KEN. Oh, I'm sorry. *(Lois examines the dress.)*
JAN. He has every breed imaginable. Angora.

LOIS. You've already ruined my life, what's a dress? *(Lois starts for the terrace again.)* I've got to find out what's going on!
JAN. Persian. Siamese. Burmese.
KEN. If the cops are down there, you could be seen.
LOIS. One quick peek?
JAN. British short hair.
KEN. No. Is it torn?
LOIS. Just the hem. Don't worry about it.
JAN. Tom ... Alley.
KEN. *(To Jan.)* Stop mumbling, for Christ's sake. Get her a needle and thread. The police notice little things like that.
LOIS. It's been at least fifteen minutes! What could be going on down there? *(Jan brings needle and thread, sits down. Lois starts to repair the torn hem. Ken sticks his finger in the cassoulet.)*
KEN. This is ice cold!
LOIS. You're hungry?
KEN. I keep telling you it's the little details that trip you up.
JAN. You really think the police are going to come in here and feel the food?
KEN. You can't be too careful.
LOIS. Life isn't a detective novel.
KEN. You keep that attitude and you'll blow it, Lois.
LOIS. You think Sherlock Holmes is on his way over? Forget it.
KEN. A man's been ... A man's dead.
LOIS. Do you know how much time the average homicide investigation takes? It's too bad Al didn't get to make his presentation. You could have used the information. *(She points to Al's flip chart.)* Look it up, it's on one of those cards.
JAN. Oh my God Almighty!
KEN. What's the matter?
JAN. The meeting! We were supposed to be at Linda Selig's almost an hour ago.
KEN. I completely forgot. Christ, why would we just be sitting here letting Al sulk on the terrace if we were late for the meeting?

LOIS. Well, we could hardly go without him, since it was his show.
JAN. I wonder why they haven't called. *(She rises, goes to phone.)*
KEN. But to keep them waiting. All those people. And that cop! Why didn't *we* call? *(Jan holds up phone cord.)*
JAN. Look. The phone came out of the hickey.
KEN. It must've happened when she called Pan Am. *(Jan starts to plug it in.)* No, leave it the way it is.
JAN. But they're probably trying to reach us right now.
KEN. So? The phone accidentally came out of the hickey.
JAN. Who'd believe that?
KEN. It's the truth, goddamit! It's practically the only part of our story that is. We might as well use it.
LOIS. So I'll stick to my story that we thought the best thing to do was let him cool off? Please, I've memorized it.
JAN. What if they send somebody over?
KEN. All we know is, Al's out on the terrace.
JAN. And we don't know the phone's disconnected?
KEN. Right.
JAN. If you say so. *(Jan drops the phone cord and returns to the table.)*
LOIS. How long has it been now?
KEN. Look, you two, relax. The worst is over.
JAN. For Al, maybe. Not for us.
KEN. Let's rehearse again. It'll pass the time.
LOIS. Oh, God.
JAN. Again? We've already done it twice.
KEN. One more time. The buzzer rings. BZZZZZ. *(Jan goes to intercom, looks at Ken.)* BZZZZZ.
JAN. *(Calmly.)* Yes?
KEN. The police are here to see you, Mrs. Miller.
JAN. "The police? Really? Well, send them up."
KEN. Good! Now several minutes pass. The doorbell rings. You open the door. Now, I'm a cop. "Is there a Mrs. Alfred Shields here?"
JAN. "Why, yes. Lois, they're here to see you."
LOIS. Shit!

JAN. Shit?
KEN. Shit? What do you mean, shit? They've checked his I.D. They're looking for you. And your line is: "The police? For me?" Then you leap to your feet.
LOIS. I know the line. "The police? For me?" I'm so nervous I pricked myself with the goddamn needle.
KEN. You didn't get blood on your dress, did you?
LOIS. No, I didn't. How can you stand living with him?
KEN. Bloodstains are the first thing they look for!
JAN. On her hem?
LOIS. And you're telling *us* to relax?
KEN. Now the cop says there's been an accident, something like that.
JAN. "You mean, in the building?" *(They look at Lois.)*
KEN. Lois!
LOIS. "Oh my God, Al's out on the terrace."
KEN. Then I go to the terrace. "Jesus, he's not out here!" *(They look at Lois.)* Lois!
LOIS. What?
KEN and JAN. You missed your cue!
LOIS. Sorry. *(Lois screams. Jan rushes to her.)*
JAN. "Oh, Lois, come and sit down."
LOIS. "It's my fault. I never should have let him go out there alone."
JAN. "We should have known, too. He was so upset."
KEN. Not bad. It's just getting worse. You have to pick up your cues, Lois. Let's take it from: "You mean, in the building?"
JAN. No more.
LOIS. That's it for me, too.
KEN. Look, this has to go like clockwork. Everything depends on those first few minutes. And what about all the other stuff we went over? What to say if they say it's suicide, how the argument started ...
JAN. Don't worry. We can handle it. *(They resume their seats at the table.)*
LOIS. How much longer are we going to wait?
KEN. Ten more minutes. Then it would be about time for

us to investigate.
JAN. Let's talk about something else till they get here. *(A pause.)*
KEN. I didn't realize he'd put on weight.
LOIS. That's something else?
KEN. I just said he got heavy, that's all.
JAN. You should talk, the way you were huffing and puffing, carrying him.
LOIS. And that groan as you pushed him over.
KEN. I didn't groan.
LOIS. *(To Jan.)* Did you ... ?
JAN. No.
KEN. *(To Lois.)* I thought it was you. It sounded like it came from you.
LOIS. That was a *male* groan. It had to be you. Who else ...?
KEN and LOIS. He was still alive!
LOIS. Oh, my God!
JAN. That's impossible. Isn't it? I mean, he *looked* dead.
LOIS. What about all those people who used to be buried alive?
JAN. That was before embalming.
LOIS. Oh, my God, we killed him.
JAN. You can't kill somebody twice.
KEN. She's right. *We* killed him.
LOIS. Now, wait a minute. All I did was help you.
KEN. Dispose of the body. Except it wasn't a body yet.
LOIS. *I* killed Al?
JAN. What counts in a court of law is intent to kill.
LOIS. That's right. We thought he was dead.
JAN. When *you* killed him, you thought he was alive.
LOIS. Which makes you the actual murderer.
JAN. When the real murder happened, we were innocent bystanders.
KEN. Only the real murder happened later.
LOIS. I remember now. I did groan. Like this. *(She imitates a male groan.)*
JAN. That was it! That was what I heard!

KEN. We *all* killed him!
LOIS. You killed him both times! That makes you twice as guilty as us!
KEN. What difference does it make anyway? If he'd survived the first accident, he could've spent years as a vegetable.
LOIS. I suppose you could look at it that way.
KEN. It would have been awful for you.
JAN. He said you'd say that! That there was a bright side to murder. And you just did.
KEN. Don't get morbid. Al's gone. We've got to think of ourselves now. *(The intercom buzzes. They all leap from their chairs. It buzzes again.)* Down! Down! Sit down! *(To Jan.)* Not you! Get it! *(She doesn't move.)* Will you for God's sake answer it! *(Ken pushes her. She half rises, falls over her chair, stumbles to the door. Just as she reaches the intercom, it buzzes again. She depresses the button, by now in utter panic.)*
JAN. *(To intercom, without waiting.)* "The police? Really? Well, send them up."
VOICE SQUAWK. Mrs. Miller, is that you? What did you say?
JAN. *(Recovering.)* Greeley. I asked if it was Mr. Greeley. Mr. Maurice Greeley. We're expecting him.
VOICE SQUAWK. There's nobody by that name, Mrs. Miller.
JAN. Well, *whoever* it is, send them up! *(She returns to the table.)* I'm sorry. Everything just went out of my head.
LOIS. Christ, I wet myself.
KEN. *(Panicked.)* Let's keep our heads! Let's keep our heads! We'll get through this! Let's keep our heads!
LOIS. But what am I going to do? I wet myself!
KEN. Don't stand up till you find out he's dead!
LOIS. You're supposed to cry, not wet yourself.
KEN. *(To Jan.)* How are *you*?
JAN. I think the worst is over. In fact, I feel pretty calm. *(She hands Lois a napkin.)* It'll help it dry.
LOIS. Who's Maurice Greeley?
JAN. Didn't you get it? It sounds like "police, really?" I thought it was a pretty good recovery.

KEN. What if they ask who he is?
JAN. We'll say he's a friend of a friend — in town from Cleveland.
KEN. You *are* pretty cool all of a sudden.
JAN. It's like I went through some kind of baptism of fire. War must be like this.
KEN. I know. That's how I felt earlier.
LOIS. That's fine for you two. You didn't pee all over yourself. *(The doorbell rings. Jan goes to the door, checks the peephole.)*
JAN. Maurice Greeley?
GRANT. *(From outside.)* No. My name is Grant. Listen, let me in. *(Jan unlocks the locks and chains, opens the door and sees Grant, an officer in his twenties, in uniform. He enters. Lois panics at the sight of the uniform and screams. Everyone turns to her.)*
LOIS. "The police? For me?"
JAN. *(Thrown.)* "You mean, in the building?"
KEN. "Oh, my God. Al's out on the terrace."
LOIS. Shit! I mean, "Oh, my God, Al's out on the terrace." No, I mean, "Jesus, he's not out here." Is that it?
JAN. "Oh, Lois, come sit down."
LOIS. I am sitting down! You know I can't get up! *(Ken runs to terrace.)*
KEN. "Jesus, he's not out here."
LOIS. "We should've known." *(At a loss for words, Lois screams again.)* Oh, I know. "It's my fault. I never should have let him go out there alone."
JAN. We should've known, too. *(Ken goes outside, searching the terrace.)*
KEN. Al! Al!
LOIS. "Oh, no. Not that."
JAN. "Are you telling us he's down there — on the street?"
LOIS. "Oh, no. Not that."
KEN. "Suicide? I can't accept that."
LOIS. "I did this to him. It was my fault. My fault."
JAN. "You mustn't blame yourself."
LOIS. "I should've known. The way he's been."

KEN. "It was our fault as much as yours. I just never thought." This is Mrs. Shields. She can't get up. She's in shock. I'm Ken Miller.
LOIS. That's good. I can't get up, I'm in shock.
KEN. "We don't know what happened, Officer. He excused himself and went out onto the terrace. Then we continued with dinner. Then you arrived."
GRANT. Would you all please ...
JAN. *(Interrupts.)* "You'd better tell him the truth, Ken."
LOIS. The truth?
KEN. "There was a scene." *(Lois slides her chair toward Grant.)*
LOIS. "My husband hasn't been himself lately, Officer. His brother was killed and he — well, he just changed."
KEN. "He was killed by a mugger."
LOIS. *(Briskly.)* "He got very disagreeable, very hard to take. We lost most of our friends. I think Al was having problems at work, too. He picked a fight with Mr. Miller. And then I told him to go out there and cool off. See, it *was* my fault."
KEN. "It was always the same. About street crime. And then he got abusive." *(Grant looks at Jan, as if for help.)* She's Mrs. Miller.
LOIS. Yes. "Jan Miller. We've been friends for many years."
JAN. How do you do? "He was horrible tonight. Worse than I've ever seen him."
KEN. "He got very personal. He said those drawings were no good. He referred to them as crap." I would call that abusive. Wouldn't you?
LOIS. The phone came out of the hickey! We don't know it.
JAN. That must be why Linda never called. You must be *her* cop. *(Jan plugs the phone into the wall. It rings. She answers it.)* Hello. Oh, Linda, it's you. You won't believe this. The phone came out of the hickey. The policeman just discovered it. *(A pause.)* Yes, I know we're an hour late. But, you see, something — came up. Al's dead. *(A pause.)* He was

the one who was going to give the Crimebusters presentation. *(A pause.)* Well, it's all kind of confusing, but he seems to have gone off the terrace. We didn't know until the policeman told us. *(A pause.)* Yes, our terrace. Look, Linda, the policeman's here and we're trying to straighten it out. Yes, Linda, I'll tell her. Thank you. *(She hangs up the phone.)* That was Linda. She sends her condolences.
GRANT.   Look, I'm not ...
JAN.   *(Interrupts.)* I know. You're not Maurice Greeley.
KEN.   She thought you were him when you got here. We don't know him.
JAN.   He's a friend of a friend, in town from Cleveland.
KEN.   Shaker Heights.
JAN.   He called and we said to drop by.
LOIS.   He's not here yet. He may not even show up. You know how people from Cleveland are.
GRANT.   Look, I have to ...
LOIS.   *(Interrupts.)* "We were having dinner when the argument started." *(Grant looks at the table.)*
KEN.   It's cold!
JAN.   My husband has a thing about hot food. I always serve everything lukewarm. Ahh! *(Jan spots the blood-stained napkin that had covered Al's face, bringing it to Grant's attention.)*
GRANT.   What's that?
LOIS.   It's mine. I pricked my finger.
JAN.   She's practically a hemophiliac.
LOIS.   I pee a lot. I mean, I bleed a lot. Anyway, we thought we'd just let him go out there and cool off and he must have accidentally fallen off the pepper mill.
GRANT.   What?
JAN.   We picked it up in the islands. It's irreplaceable. *(Lois panics completely, rushes to couch.)*
LOIS.   *(Without examining anything.)* "This is my husband's coat. Oh look, there's a package in the pocket. What are all these checks? Al left the agency."
KEN.   *(Despairing.)* "And with quite a lot of money."
LOIS.   This proves it. He *was* crazy.

GRANT. What are —?
LOIS. *(Interrupts.)* Well, why would he close the bank accounts and the money market fund and then jump off the balcony? I mean, fall. Anyway, he *had* to be out of his mind!
JAN. Lois!
LOIS. It's obvious. You don't convert all your assets to cash and then ... *(She realizes what she's said.)* He didn't ask? Well, I just assumed. I mean, there was more than one check. So naturally, I ... *(To Grant.)* Why are you browbeating me like this? My husband is dead down there! You think I did it. They did it!
JAN. Oh my God Almighty!
KEN. *(To Jan.)* I told you we shouldn't have tried to cover up for her. But no, you had to protect your best friend!
LOIS. They did it! They did it!
KEN. I'm sorry, Lois. We've gone as far as we can for you.
JAN. She killed him with the pepper mill. Right in front of our eyes. It was awful.
KEN. Then she pushed his body off the terrace.
JAN. She begged us not to tell.
KEN. I wanted to call the police. But I had two hysterical women on my hands.
LOIS. They made *me* cover up for *them!* It's a trick.
GRANT. They made you do what?
LOIS. They made me touch the pepper mill after *he* killed him with it and *she* cleaned off his fingerprints. Oh, I know it sound ridiculous, but it's true. *She* killed him, too. Later.
JAN. She's obviously insane.
LOIS. The second time we killed him! I mean the second time *he* killed him. We only killed him once.
KEN. You see? She's crazy. *(To Jan.)* Maybe we'd better tell him the whole truth, honey, and get it over with.
JAN. I suppose we'd better. I'm sorry, Lois.
LOIS. It's a lie. It's a lie! They're going to tell you she had an affair with my husband. *(Grant looks at Ken.)* No, *my*

husband.
KEN. Mrs. Shields found out tonight. That's why she killed him. It was horrible.
JAN. I'm so ashamed.
LOIS. It's a goddamned, stinking lie. *(She stops cold.)* Will somebody tell me why he isn't saying anything? *(Grant tries to speak, Jan interrupts.)*
JAN. She's right. He hasn't said a word since he came in.
KEN. Hold on. Are you the Seligs' cop or not?
JAN. Did Linda Selig ...?
GRANT. Who —
LOIS. *(Interrupts.)* He's a regular cop. They must've found Al and called 9-1-1 from the lobby. *(To Jan.)* This is your fault, leaping to conclusions about the phone hickey! You always were weak-minded.
KEN. Where are you from?
GRANT. I'm from —
JAN. *(Interrupts.)* I'm weak-minded? You just blew the whole thing. And you call *me* weak-minded? *(Grant points upward.)*
LOIS. The new building?
JAN. Nobody lives there yet! *(Ken goes to Grant, examines a narrow blue arm patch on his uniform.)*
KEN. "Metropolitan Security." Christ, he's a security guard over there. *(To Jan.)* You should have done something about those windows!
LOIS. Oh, my God, he saw us kill him.
KEN. Keep quiet!
JAN. But what happened to the real cops?
GRANT. The body hasn't been discovered yet. People figure he's just another derelict, I guess. One old lady gave him some change.
JAN. *(To Ken.)* Ask him why he's here.
KEN. He wants to blackmail us. Why else would he be here?
LOIS. Blackmail. Oh, how contemptible.
JAN. *(To Ken.)* Ask him how much he wants.
KEN. *(To Grant)* Fifteen thousand. Take it or leave it. *(Grant*

goes to the phone.)
LOIS. I think he's leaving it. *(Grant dials three digits.)*
KEN. Twenty!
GRANT. *(Into phone.)* Police? This is Officer Allen C. Grant, Metropolitan Security.
KEN. Forty thousand. That's it!
JAN. That's all we've got!
GRANT. There's been a man killed —
LOIS. Sixty!
GRANT. — at 415 East Fifty-second street. No, East. No, Fifty-second, Five — two. Look, the body's down on the sidewalk. I'm in apartment 10-C. Thank you. *(He hangs up.)* They should be here in about ten minutes.
KEN. What are you going to say when they get here?
LOIS. What do you think he's going to say? He's going to tell them everything he saw. Everything. The murder. Tampering with the evidence. Attempting to conceal a crime. The second murder. Everything!
GRANT. You're wrong, Mrs. — Miller, is it?
LOIS. What?
KEN. You mean you're not going to tell?
GRANT. No. I mean I didn't see any of that.
JAN. What?
KEN. What did you see?
GRANT. I saw the body on the sidewalk. I saw you three having dinner like nothing had happened. I figured it would be the decent thing to break the news to you before the cops showed up.
LOIS. New York's only Good Samaritan and we had to get him.
JAN. Then why didn't you tell us?
LOIS. *(Interrupts.)* Because you wouldn't let him get a word —
JAN. *(Interrupts.)* He could have interrupted. Besides, you were —
GRANT. *(Interrupts.)* What did happen here? *(He indicates Lois.)* Is what she said true?
KEN. Well, in a way, yes. But she didn't mention that he

had a gun.
JAN.   It's right here in his jacket.
KEN.   He was going to kill me with it.
LOIS.   He was going to kill us all, we think.
JAN.   He was actually hiding in that chest. *(Grant opens the chest, picks up the lingerie.)*
LOIS.   He was a very sick man. *(Grant takes the gun from Al's jacket, examines it.)*
GRANT.   That makes it self-defense. Why didn't you just call the cops?
KEN.   I've never even had a parking ticket. I was afraid I'd go to jail.
GRANT.   If what you're saying is true, you'll get off. Your attorney will have you out on bail in the morning.
JAN.   Do you really think so?
GRANT.   Sure. Aggravated assault with a deadly weapon. A history of weird behavior. *(He drops the lingerie into the chest.)* Two witnesses. You're all well dressed. No problem. *(He closes the chest.)*
KEN.   You seem to know a lot about it.
GRANT.   I only do this at night. I'm a law student.
KEN.   You're working your way through law school?
GRANT.   That's right.
KEN.   As a night security guard. Must be a pretty tough schedule.
GRANT.   It's not easy.
KEN.   But I guess if you have to, you have to.
GRANT.   I don't have to, really. My old man's the general contractor on the building.
KEN.   And he got you the job. He's trying to build your character, huh?
GRANT.   Yeah. He's a real shmuck.
KEN.   I'm going to ask you something, and I don't want you to be offended by it. Okay?
GRANT.   Okay.
KEN.   You're a law student. Does that mean you believe in justice?
GRANT.   I guess so.

KEN. And isn't justice, in laymen's terms, just people getting what they deserve?
GRANT. When the system works.
KEN. That's what I'm talking about. It doesn't anymore, not very often. And if it doesn't in my case, I face a prison sentence. Is that what I deserve?
GRANT. I guess not.
KEN. For that matter, is it fair that a nice, bright kid like you has to work nights in a rotten menial job to put himself through school? Don't you deserve better than that?
GRANT. Now wait a minute here.
JAN. He's right, Allen.
LOIS. Why shouldn't they spend their money on something worthwhile instead of handing it over to crooked lawyers?
GRANT. You want me to blackmail my way through law school?
KEN. Why don't we think of it as a student loan?
JAN. You deserve a better life, Allen. You're a nice kid.
LOIS. And you'd be giving them a chance to make up for what they did.
JAN. Why don't you give him that chance?
KEN. A student loan. You could even pay it back someday, if you like.
JAN. Although you wouldn't have to.
GRANT. You actually make it sound like the right thing to do.
KEN. It is, Allen. For all of us.
JAN. Oh, yes, Allen, it is.
GRANT. All right. I'll go along with it.
JAN. Thank you, Allen.
KEN. You'll never regret this.
LOIS. What will you tell the police?
KEN. Just what he saw. The body on the sidewalk and he came over to tell us. Oh, boy, now we've got a *witness* who didn't see us do it!
LOIS. There's one thing I don't understand, though, and maybe the cops won't either. How did you know he came

from this apartment?
KEN. Yeah, how did you?
GRANT. Where else would he come from?
KEN. What do you mean?
GRANT. He did live here, didn't he? *(Grant looks at Jan as she indicates "no.")* I mean, him and you? *(He points to the bedroom, Jan looks away.)* He wasn't your husband? *(Jan gets up, sees Lois and crosses away.)* Oh, wow! *(Lois goes to phone, dials.)*
KEN. What are you doing, Lois? Lois! Who are you calling? Lois! *(Lois furiously hums "New York, New York" as she waits for her call to be answered.)*
LOIS. *(Into phone.)* Hello, Pan Am? I want to confirm my reservation on your flight to Rio tomorrow. That's it, 304. My name is Jan Miller. *(A pause.)* I'm confirmed. Thank you so much, Pan Am. *(She hangs up, advances toward Jan.)* "Maybe my style is changing."
JAN. There's been a mistake.
LOIS. "Would you be more content without Al?"
JAN. A terrible mistake.
LOIS. "The last time he was here, he was pretty well behaved." I'll bet. Sweet, loveable, wholesome Jan — the husband humper! *(She grabs Jan by the throat. They struggle, scattering ashtrays, glasses, etc., to the floor.)*
GRANT. Come on now, you two, cut it out! *(He separates the two women.)*
KEN. You and Al? Al?
LOIS. My best friend!
KEN. Al *Shields*? That asshole?
JAN. He was not an asshole.
LOIS. Oh, yeah?
KEN. Why him, of all people?
JAN. He was interested in me!
KEN. Interested in you?
JAN. Yes, interested in me, believe it or not. As something more than a messenger to shlep his crummy drawings to the framers.
LOIS. What he was interested in was an easy lay. He always was.

JAN. Only because he had to be! The closest you ever came to enjoying sex was listening to me do it through a keyhole. So what's to complain about? At least two out of the four of us had a sex life!
LOIS. Complete with kinky nightgowns. And God knows what else you've got hidden around here in the way of sex toys.
GRANT. Like the mask.
KEN. The mask?
GRANT. The little black one made with feathers.
LOIS. Oh my God, how disgusting!
GRANT. They used to take turns playing "Dangerous Intruder."
JAN. He's making it up! I swear. He's making it up!
KEN. In my home? While I was working late at that lousy office to support you?
LOIS. And this cozy little get-together tonight. What was that, your going-away party?
JAN. He thought it might look suspicious if he turned Ken down. He even made me go to that audition.
KEN. A mask?
GRANT. Cut it out, folks.
KEN. Now just a minute, pal. Who do —
GRANT. *(Interrupts.)* CUT IT OUT! You got that?
KEN. I don't have to —
GRANT. *(Interrupts.)* YOU GOT THAT!!
KEN. I got it.
GRANT. The cops'll be here any minute. Let's do the deal.
LOIS. What deal?
GRANT. The blackmail deal.
LOIS. Sorry. I keep losing track of what crime we're committing.
KEN. All right, Allen. We'll get you a nice little apartment somewhere, your food, your books.
GRANT. Little apartment? Food? Books? She said I deserve a better life.
KEN. Okay, the fifteen thousand.
GRANT. That's not a better life, Ken. That's a better

month.
KEN. What do you want?
GRANT. More.
KEN. We're not rich.
GRANT. Too bad. Things are expensive in prison. Cigarettes. Candy bars. Gang rape insurance.
KEN. Gang rape insurance?
GRANT. You can't play softball twenty-four hours a day.
KEN. How much more?
GRANT. Everything.
KEN. Everything?
JAN. *(To Ken.)* What does he mean, everything?
LOIS. I think he means everything, right down to the gold fillings.
GRANT. I just want my fair share. My large fair share. We'll go over all the assets tomorrow. Tomorrow night. I have some shopping to do in the afternoon, after I quit my rotten menial job.
JAN. All we have is forty thousand dollars. That's all. Forty thousand dollars.
LOIS. Will you for Christ's sake stop saying that? You sound like a public television fund drive.
JAN. You've both forgotten something. It's just his word against ours. The word of a self-admitted voyeur. *(Grants turns on, rewinds, then plays the tape recorder.)*
AL'S VOICE. "Woof."
GRANT. Wrong. *(He fast-forwards the tape.)*
LOIS' VOICE. "Why are you browbeating me like this? My husband is dead down there! You think I did it. They did it!" *(Grant fast-forwards the tape again.)*
JAN'S VOICE. "She killed him with the pepper —" *(He turns off the recorder, puts the cassette in his jacket pocket.)*
KEN. You saw everything, didn't you? Right from the beginning?
GRANT. But then I spotted this. And I figured, with taped confessions, I could do a lot better than fifteen grand. By the way, what's the name of your travel agent? I'll be needing a little vacation after we clear this mess up. Some-

where warm, and wonderful. Antigua might be nice. I don't think it's been completely ruined yet.
JAN. *(To Ken.)* We can't afford this.
KEN. You want to go to jail? I can get more commissions, and you can get more commercials. *(He indicates Lois.)* God knows she has plenty.
LOIS. I'll pay one third and that's all.
KEN. How do you think you came into all your money?
LOIS. I'm supposed to be grateful? Because you murdered my husband? After she fucked his brains out?
GRANT. Hey folks, cool it. You people have to learn to stick together. Play as a team. It's the only way you're going to get out of this. Now listen to me carefully. My story is I was making my rounds and I saw this guy acting strange out on your terrace. Talking to himself, gesturing. A little drunk, wobbly. He was pacing up and down, then he tripped or something and went over the side. Then I came over and told you, like I said before. They'll buy it. The problem is will you be able to keep it straight when they get here? If they ever do.
KEN. No wonder the city's going down the drain. *(Grant removes his jacket, places it over back of sofa.)*
GRANT. Do you really think more efficient police work would make this sewer livable? Face it, Ken, it's all over here. Don't you know what's out there, on the street? Subhumans, crazies, drug addicts, and muggers. Most of them will rob you, then kill you for the fun of it. That's what's left in New York, except for victims. Anybody with sense moved to Larchmont years ago.
LOIS. Sort of takes you back, doesn't it?
GRANT. What's that mean?
LOIS. It means I could use a drink. *(She goes to bar.)* Anybody else?
KEN. Fix me a Scotch, will you? A very large one.
JAN. Me, too.
GRANT. No.
LOIS. What do you mean, no?
GRANT. I mean no. You have enough trouble keeping

your stories straight as it is. *(He goes to bar.)* Where's the good stuff?
KEN. That's all there is. *(Grant fixes a drink.)*
GRANT. Domestic vodka? Order a case of that Polish stuff tomorrow. And some Glenfiddich. *(He looks around.)* How come everything's practically the same color in here? It looks like a dentist's waiting room. Have it painted. Aubergine might be nice. And buy new furniture. Italian, maybe. Something with a little style. I'll be wanting to have people over. *(He looks at Ken's drawings.)* And get rid of those. What are they anyway?
LOIS. They're Ken's. He drew them, I mean.
GRANT. Oh, you're an architect. Boy, this stuff is real shit. You must make a fortune. *(To Lois.)* How about you? What do you do?
LOIS. I'm a book editor.
GRANT. Anybody I ever heard of?
KEN. Arthur Weller.
GRANT. More shit. More big bucks. Nice. *(To Jan.)* And I've been watching you in commercials for years. Didn't recognize you at first. Then one night I happened to look over here and catch you with your clothes on. Looks like I have pulled together a fine little group of wage earners. Tell you what. Let's go over the story until they get here. Gotta protect all that income.
LOIS. Oh, my God, not again.
GRANT. If there's one thing I can't stand, it's a mouthy woman. That type, they get tired of a husband, they'd just as soon shove him off a terrace as look at him. Best place for a woman like that is prison.
LOIS. I'm sorry.
GRANT. Good. You're learning. Now, the story.
LOIS. You were making your rounds. *(Grant looks at Jan.)*
JAN. You saw him on the terrace. He looked drunk, wobbly. *(Grant looks at Ken.)*
KEN. Then he tripped and went over the side. You saw us sitting here having dinner like we didn't know what —
GRANT. *(Interrupts.)* Damn. It won't work.

KEN. Why not?
GRANT. The railing, Ken. You don't trip over a fucking railing unless you're eleven feet tall.
LOIS. Why don't we just go back to Plan A? You saw him on the sidewalk and came over.
GRANT. No, it's neater if I saw him fall. That way it's all tied up for them. The less questions they have to ask you people the better.
KEN. I know! What if the railing was loose?
GRANT. Not bad. Not bad at all. This is a pretty old building. It might work. And we could sue, couldn't we? Oh, I like this.
KEN. I'll just pry it away from the wall. It's kind of shaky anyway. It'll only take a minute.
GRANT. No. I'll take care of it. I want it done right. *(Grant exits onto the terrace, begins prying the railing loose. Jan, Lois and Ken exchange a look, then exit onto the terrace. They grab Grant from behind, throw him over. Jan, Lois and Ken enter from the terrace.)*
JAN. Well, he told us to stick together.
KEN. We don't have time for that. The police could be here any minute.
LOIS. Could we please make sure it's really them this time?
JAN. I'm a little confused. What's our story now?
KEN. We'll stay as close to the truth as possible, like before. What was it he said? He came over to tell us about Al before the cops showed up.
LOIS. But didn't he tell them we did it when he called them?
JAN. No, he said there'd been a man *killed* and the body was on the sidewalk.
KEN. He could have meant accidentally.
LOIS. Then what happened?
KEN. Then he took us out on the terrace to show us how the accident happened.
JAN. And it happened again. Oh, that's good.
KEN. Does everything in the room fit this story?

57

JAN. No. It wouldn't be messed up because Lois and I didn't have a fight now, right? *(They pick up magazines, ashtrays, glasses, etc., put the gun back.)*
KEN. Everything should be just as it was before he got here. Exactly the way it was. *(Jan notices Grant's uniform jacket just as Lois and Ken notice the bloody napkin under the table.)* We'd better get rid of that. *(Jan nods agreement, picks up Grant's jacket and exits onto terrace. Lois picks up the napkin.)*
LOIS. What'll we do with it?
KEN. We'll spread it flat under the rug and we can get rid of it in the morning. *(They do so as Jan enters from the terrace, without the jacket.)*
JAN. Oh, my God. Woof!
LOIS. What?
KEN. The cassette. Thank God you remembered.
LOIS. That's right. It has all the confessions to everything on it. *(Ken goes to cassette player, opens it.)*
KEN. Where can we hide — It isn't in here! It isn't in here!
LOIS. Of course it's in there. I heard it. "They did it. They did it."
JAN. Didn't he take it out after he played it for us?
LOIS. Yes, he did. I remember. But where did he put it?
JAN. I know! He put it in his — *(She turns toward the terrace.)* — jacket.
LOIS. Where is it?
KEN. Did you hang it up?
LOIS. I said where is it? Jan? What's the matter with you?
KEN. What did you do with the goddamn thing?
JAN. You said everything should be just as it was before he got here. Well, the jacket got here when he did!
KEN. *(Horrified.)* You threw it — over?
LOIS. You mean it's down there? With the bodies? You threw our confessions off the terrace? I mean your confessions. How could I confess to anything? I didn't do anything. *(To Jan.)* He killed him and you helped him cover it up.
KEN. What about the second time we killed him? And what about Grant? That was your idea!
LOIS. I was an innocent bystander the whole time. I'll

just tell them the truth, that's what I'll do. *(Suddenly she is talking to the police.)* He murdered my husband in cold blood, Officer. Then the two of them threatened to kill me if I didn't help them cover it up.
KEN. You want the real truth, Officer? She found out he was having an affair with my wife and bashed him with that pepper mill. Her finger prints are all over it.
LOIS. Then that poor security guard came over to rescue me — he'd witnessed the whole thing — and they got him too.
KEN. He saw it all right, but he came over to help *us*, and she bashed him. Then she threw both bodies off the terrace. I've heard the insane have incredible strength, but I'd never seen it before.
JAN. What if it was all a game?
LOIS. Be careful, Officer, they're on automatic now. Whoever shows up in a uniform, they murder. If a Girl Scout came to the door selling cookies, she'd be over the side before she knew what hit her. What do you mean, a game?
JAN. One of those board games. Like Monopoly. Or Trivial Pursuits.
KEN. What?
JAN. You're always trying to invent one, in your spare time. It's a little hobby of yours. Don't you remember?
KEN. Oh. What was this game like?
JAN. It was a murder game. You know, like a mystery novel. The players are assigned different roles. Murder, victim, detective. That's why all this stuff is on the tape. You recorded it so you could work out the flaws later.
LOIS. But why was Grant here?
JAN. He invented games too. I got to talking to him down on the street one day and he told me. So I invited him over.
KEN. But we were going to the Seligs.
JAN. He dropped in unexpectedly, and we didn't want to be rude. So we decided to play one quick game.
LOIS. But how did they —? *(She makes the diving gesture.)*
JAN. Together.
LOIS. Together?

KEN. Arm-in-Arm?
JAN. They started quarrelling. Over the game.
KEN. Al would do that.
JAN. And they got into a fight. A fist fight! *(The intercom buzzes. Jan starts to mess up the room again.)* A real brawl, knocking things over, rolling around on the floor.
KEN. Punching, kicking. *(The intercom buzzes.)*
JAN. And finally they ended up —
KEN. Out there!
JAN. And over they went.
KEN. Honey, you're wonderful!
LOIS. But didn't he give them his name?
KEN. Didn't who give who his name?
LOIS. What's-his-name, the one we just —. Didn't he give the police his name when he called to say Al went over?
KEN. She's right. They couldn't have gone over together. *(The intercom buzzes, keeps buzzing.)*
JAN. You think they got his name right? They probably didn't even get the address right. Look how long it took them to get here.
KEN. But I think they tape those calls.
JAN. Look, if it comes up, we'll wing it. *(She goes to the intercom.)* Like we always do. *(To intercom, after depressing button.)* Yes?
VOICE SQUAWK. Mrs. Miller?
JAN. Yes.
VOICE SQUAWK. Mrs. Miller, it's about this security guard. *(A pause.)*
JAN. Yes?
VOICE SQUAWK. He says he wants to come up.
JAN. Up?
VOICE SQUAWK. Yeah. He says he's tired of waiting down here for his buddy and he wants to come up. He wants you to ask the other security guard if it's okay now.
JAN. The other security guard?
VOICE SQUAWK. The one I sent up before. They work together. Across the street.
JAN. Oh. I see.

VOICE SQUAWK. So what should I do.
JAN. Do?
VOICE SQUAWK. Yeah. Like I been saying. He wants to know if you people are ready for him now.
JAN. Oh. *(To Ken and Lois.)* Are we ready for him? *(Ken wearily picks up the pepper mill, using a napkin. Lois slides open the terrace door. They nod. To intercom.)* Yes. We're ready for him.

THE END

PROPERTY LIST

Keys (Jan and Ken)
Shopping bag for lingerie (Jan)
Shopping bag for cassoulet (Jan)
Lingerie (Jan)
Cassoulet (Jan)
Tote bag (Lois)
Jewelry (Lois)
Dress shoes (Lois)
Credit card (Al)
Old army coat (Lois)
Framed architectural drawings wrapped in paper (Jan)
Presentation case with flip chart (Al)
Tape recorder with tape (Al)
Blueprint canister (Ken)
Vase
Wine Glasses
Fruit bowls
Plates
Butter dish
Butter knives
Forks
Spoons
Serving spoons
Bread basket
Silver serving trays
Small plate
Wine bottle with cork
Wine bottle opener
Scotch bottle
Vodka bottle
Coffee pot
Trivet
Cassoulet dish
Pot holders

Ice bucket
Tongs
Drinking glasses
Pepper mill approximately 2 ft. long
Magazines
Containers for food
Cream cheese
Butter
Celery
Rolls
Fruit salad
Grape juice (for wine)
Tea bags (for Scotch)
Water (for Vodka)
Coffee
Napkins
Gun with small holder
Sewing basket with thread, needle and pin cushion
Bloody napkin
Envelope with folder papers:
    cashier's check
    letter of resignation
    insurance policy
    money market check
    savings account check
    slip of paper with "PA 304, 9734000"

COSTUME PLOT

JAN

Cobalt blue sweater
Blue/purple bouclé skirt
Black textured hosiery
Black leather pumps
Lavendar trenchcoat
Yellow/bronze bracelet
Blue/gold earrings
Blue/purple bauble necklaces
Wedding rings

LOIS

Black suit with velvet trim
Blouse
Black rubber boots
Plaid scarf
Beat-up overcoat
Black grosgrain pumps
Sheer black hosiery
Gold chain jewelry
"Pearl" and gold earrings

AL

Ochre/black striped shirt
Bow tie
Sweater vest
Herringbone slacks
Socks
Cordovan loafers
Green scarf
Army trench coat

KEN

Blue jacket
Light blue dress shirt
Red and blue striped tie
Socks
Black dress shoes
Tan pants
Camel overcoat

GRANT

Blue police shirt
Black tie
Blue police suit jacket
Police pants
Police hat
Police badge
Black belt with pouch
Socks
Black boots

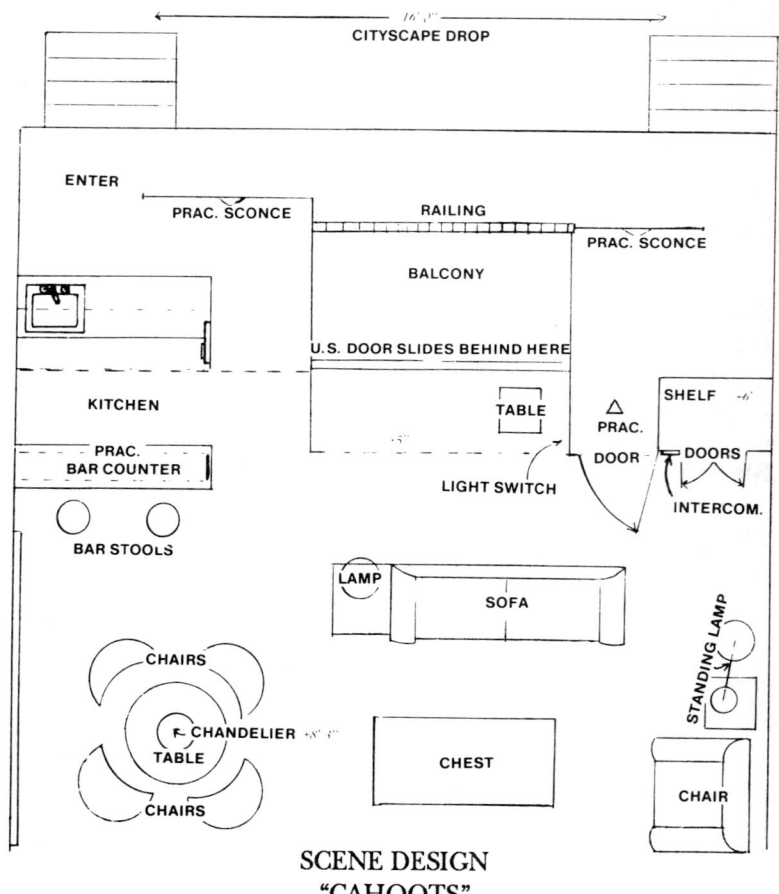

**SCENE DESIGN
"CAHOOTS"**

Designed by Scott Bradley for the
South Street Theatre Production.

NEW PLAYS

★ **HONOUR by Joanna Murray-Smith.** In a series of intense confrontations, a wife, husband, lover and daughter negotiate the forces of passion, history, responsibility and honour. "HONOUR makes for surprisingly interesting viewing. Tight, crackling dialogue (usually played out in punchy verbal duels) captures characters unable to deal with emotions ... Murray-Smith effectively places her characters in situations that strip away pretense." *−Variety* "... the play's virtues are strong: a distinctive theatrical voice, passionate concerns ... HONOUR might just capture a few honors of its own." *−Time Out Magazine* [1M, 3W] ISBN: 0-8222-1683-3

★ **MR. PETERS' CONNECTIONS by Arthur Miller.** Mr. Miller describes the protagonist as existing in a dream-like state when the mind is "freed to roam from real memories to conjectures, from trivialities to tragic insights, from terror of death to glorying in one's being alive." With this memory play, the Tony Award and Pulitzer Prize-winner reaffirms his stature as the world's foremost dramatist. "... a cross between Joycean stream-of-consciousness and Strindberg's dream plays, sweetened with a dose of William Saroyan's philosophical whimsy ... CONNECTIONS is most intriguing ..." *−The NY Times* [5M, 3W] ISBN: 0-8222-1687-6

★ **THE WAITING ROOM by Lisa Loomer.** Three women from different centuries meet in a doctor's waiting room in this dark comedy about the timeless quest for beauty − and its cost. "... THE WAITING ROOM ... is a bold, risky melange of conflicting elements that is ... terrifically moving ... There's no resisting the fierce emotional pull of the play." *−The NY Times* "... one of the high points of this year's Off-Broadway season ... THE WAITING ROOM is well worth a visit." *−Back Stage* [7M, 4W, flexible casting] ISBN: 0-8222-1594-2

★ **THE OLD SETTLER by John Henry Redwood.** A sweet-natured comedy about two church-going sisters in 1943 Harlem and the handsome young man who rents a room in their apartment. "For all of its decent sentiments, THE OLD SETTLER avoids sentimentality. It has the authenticity and lack of pretense of an Early American sampler." *−The NY Times* "We've had some fine plays Off-Broadway this season, and this is one of the best." *−The NY Post* [1M, 3W] ISBN: 0-8-222-1642-6

★ **THE LAST TRAIN TO NIBROC by Arlene Hutton.** In 1940 two young strangers share a seat on a train bound east only to find their paths will cross again. "All aboard. LAST TRAIN TO NIBROC is a sweetly told little chamber romance." *−Show Business* "... [a] gently charming little play, reminiscent of Thornton Wilder in its look at rustic Americans who are to be treasured for their simplicity and directness ..." *−Associated Press* "The old formula of boy wins girls, boy loses girl, boy wins girl still works ... [a] well-made play that perfectly captures a slice of small-town-life-gone-by." *−Back Stage* [1M, 1W] ISBN: 0-8222-1753-8

★ **OVER THE RIVER AND THROUGH THE WOODS by Joe DiPietro.** Nick sees both sets of his grandparents every Sunday for dinner. This is routine until he has to tell them that he's been offered a dream job in Seattle. The news doesn't sit so well. "A hilarious family comedy that is even funnier than his long running musical revue *I Love You, You're Perfect, Now Change*." *−Back Stage* "Loaded with laughs every step of the way." *−Star-Ledger* [3M, 3W] ISBN: 0-8222-1712-0

★ **SIDE MAN by Warren Leight.** 1999 Tony Award winner. This is the story of a broken family and the decline of jazz as popular entertainment. "... a tender, deeply personal memory play about the turmoil in the family of a jazz musician as his career crumbles at the dawn of the age of rock-and-roll ..." *−The NY Times* "[SIDE MAN] is an elegy for two things − a lost world and a lost love. When the two notes sound together in harmony, it is moving and graceful ..." *−The NY Daily News* "An atmospheric memory play...with crisp dialogue and clearly drawn characters ... reflects the passing of an era with persuasive insight ... The joy and despair of the musicians is skillfully illustrated." *−Variety* [5M, 3W] ISBN: 0-8222-1721-X

DRAMATISTS PLAY SERVICE, INC.
440 Park Avenue South, New York, NY 10016 212-683-8960 Fax 212-213-1539
postmaster@dramatists.com   www.dramatists.com

NEW PLAYS

★ **CLOSER by Patrick Marber.** Winner of the 1998 Olivier Award for Best Play and the 1999 New York Drama Critics Circle Award for Best Foreign Play. Four lives intertwine over the course of four and a half years in this densely plotted, stinging look at modern love and betrayal. "CLOSER is a sad, savvy, often funny play that casts a steely, unblinking gaze at the world of relationships and lets you come to your own conclusions ... CLOSER does not merely hold your attention; it burrows into you." –*New York Magazine* "A powerful, darkly funny play about the cosmic collision between the sun of love and the comet of desire." –*Newsweek Magazine* [2M, 2W] ISBN: 0-8222-1722-8

★ **THE MOST FABULOUS STORY EVER TOLD by Paul Rudnick.** A stage manager, headset and prompt book at hand, brings the house lights to half, then dark, and cues the creation of the world. Throughout the play, she's in control of everything. In other words, she's either God, or she thinks she is. "Line by line, Mr. Rudnick may be the funniest writer for the stage in the United States today ... One-liners, epigrams, withering put-downs and flashing repartee: These are the candles that Mr. Rudnick lights instead of cursing the darkness ... a testament to the virtues of laughing ... and in laughter, there is something like the memory of Eden." –*The NY Times* "Funny it is ... consistently, rapaciously, deliriously ... easily the funniest play in town." –*Variety* [4M, 5W] ISBN: 0-8222-1720-1

★ **A DOLL'S HOUSE by Henrik Ibsen, adapted by Frank McGuinness.** Winner of the 1997 Tony Award for Best Revival. "New, raw, gut-twisting and gripping. Easily the hottest drama this season." –*USA Today* "Bold, brilliant and alive." –*The Wall Street Journal* "A thunderclap of an evening that takes your breath away." –*Time Magazine* [4M, 4W, 2 boys] ISBN: 0-8222-1636-1

★ **THE HERBAL BED by Peter Whelan.** The play is based on actual events which occurred in Stratford-upon-Avon in the summer of 1613, when William Shakespeare's elder daughter was publicly accused of having a sexual liaison with a married neighbor and family friend. "In his probing new play, THE HERBAL BED ... Peter Whelan muses about a sidelong event in the life of Shakespeare's family and creates a finely textured tapestry of love and lies in the early 17th-century Stratford." –*The NY Times* "It is a first rate drama with interesting moral issues of truth and expediency." –*The NY Post* [5M, 3W] ISBN: 0-8222-1675-2

★ **SNAKEBIT by David Marshall Grant.** A study of modern friendship when put to the test. "... a rather smart and absorbing evening of water-cooler theater, the intimate sort of Off-Broadway experience that has you picking apart the recognizable characters long after the curtain calls." – *The NY Times* "Off-Broadway keeps on presenting us with compelling reasons for going to the theater. The latest is SNAKEBIT, David Marshall Grant's smart new comic drama about being thirtysomething and losing one's way in life." –*The NY Daily News* [3M, 1W] ISBN: 0-8222-1724-4

★ **A QUESTION OF MERCY by David Rabe.** The Obie Award-winning playwright probes the sensitive and controversial issue of doctor-assisted suicide in the age of AIDS in this poignant drama. "There are many devastating ironies in Mr. Rabe's beautifully considered, piercingly clear-eyed work ..." –*The NY Times* "With unsettling candor and disturbing insight, the play arouses pity and understanding of a troubling subject ... Rabe's provocative tale is an affirmation of dignity that rings clear and true." –*Variety* [6M, 1W] ISBN: 0-8222-1643-4

★ **DIMLY PERCEIVED THREATS TO THE SYSTEM by Jon Klein.** Reality and fantasy overlap with hilarious results as this unforgettable family attempts to survive the nineties. "Here's a play whose point about fractured families goes to the heart, mind – and ears." –*The Washington Post* "... an end-of-the-millennium comedy about a family on the verge of a nervous breakdown ... Trenchant and hilarious ..." –*The Baltimore Sun* [2M, 4W] ISBN: 0-8222-1677-9

DRAMATISTS PLAY SERVICE, INC.
440 Park Avenue South, New York, NY 10016 212-683-8960 Fax 212-213-1539
postmaster@dramatists.com   www.dramatists.com

NEW PLAYS

★ **AS BEES IN HONEY DROWN by Douglas Carter Beane.** Winner of the John Gassner Playwriting Award. A hot young novelist finds the subject of his new screenplay in a New York socialite who leads him into the world of *Auntie Mame* and *Breakfast at Tiffany's*, before she takes him for a ride. "A delicious soufflé of a satire ... [an] extremely entertaining fable for an age that always chooses image over substance." –*The NY Times* "... A witty assessment of one of the most active and relentless industries in a consumer society ... the creation of 'hot' young things, which the media have learned to mass produce with efficiency and zeal." –*The NY Daily News* [3M, 3W, flexible casting] ISBN: 0-8222-1651-5

★ **STUPID KIDS by John C. Russell.** In rapid, highly stylized scenes, the story follows four high-school students as they make their way from first through eighth period and beyond, struggling with the fears, frustrations, and longings peculiar to youth. "In STUPID KIDS ... playwright John C. Russell gets the opera of adolescence to a T ... The stylized teenspeak of STUPID KIDS ... suggests that Mr. Russell may have hidden a tape recorder under a desk in study hall somewhere and then scoured the tapes for good quotations ... it is the kids' insular, ceaselessly churning world, a pre-adult world of Doritos and libidos, that the playwright seeks to lay bare." –*The NY Times* "STUPID KIDS [is] a sharp-edged ... whoosh of teen angst and conformity anguish. It is also very funny." –*NY Newsday* [2M, 2W] ISBN: 0-8222-1698-1

★ **COLLECTED STORIES by Donald Margulies.** From Obie Award-winner Donald Margulies comes a provocative analysis of a student-teacher relationship that turns sour when the protégé becomes a rival. "With his fine ear for detail, Margulies creates an authentic, insular world, and he gives equal weight to the opposing viewpoints of two formidable characters." –*The LA Times* "This is probably Margulies' best play to date ..." –*The NY Post* "... always fluid and lively, the play is thick with ideas, like a stock-pot of good stew." –*The Village Voice* [2W] ISBN: 0-8222-1640-X

★ **FREEDOMLAND by Amy Freed.** An overdue showdown between a son and his father sets off fireworks that illuminate the neurosis, rage and anxiety of one family – and of America at the turn of the millennium. "FREEDOMLAND's more obvious links are to *Buried Child* and *Bosoms and Neglect*. Freed, like Guare, is an inspired wordsmith with a gift for surreal touches in situations grounded in familiar and real territory." –*Curtain Up* [3M, 4W] ISBN: 0-8222-1719-8

★ **STOP KISS by Diana Son.** A poignant and funny play about the ways, both sudden and slow, that lives can change irrevocably. "There's so much that is vital and exciting about STOP KISS ... you want to embrace this young author and cheer her onto other works ... the writing on display here is funny and credible ... you also will be charmed by its heartfelt characters and up-to-the-minute humor." –*The NY Daily News* "... irresistibly exciting ... a sweet, sad, and enchantingly sincere play." –*The NY Times* [3M, 3W] ISBN: 0-8222-1731-7

★ **THREE DAYS OF RAIN by Richard Greenberg.** The sins of fathers and mothers make for a bittersweet elegy in this poignant and revealing drama. "... a work so perfectly judged it heralds the arrival of a major playwright ... Greenberg is extraordinary." –*The NY Daily News* "Greenberg's play is filled with graceful passages that are by turns melancholy, harrowing, and often, quite funny." –*Variety* [2M, 1W] ISBN: 0-8222-1676-0

★ **THE WEIR by Conor McPherson.** In a bar in rural Ireland, the local men swap spooky stories in an attempt to impress a young woman from Dublin who recently moved into a nearby "haunted" house. However, the tables are soon turned when she spins a yarn of her own. "You shed all sense of time at this beautiful and devious new play." –*The NY Times* "Sheer theatrical magic. I have rarely been so convinced that I have just seen a modern classic. Tremendous." –*The London Daily Telegraph* [4M, 1W] ISBN: 0-8222-1706-6

DRAMATISTS PLAY SERVICE, INC.
440 Park Avenue South, New York, NY 10016 212-683-8960 Fax 212-213-1539
postmaster@dramatists.com   www.dramatists.com